CAREERS IN FILM AND TELEVISION

SO YOU WANT TO BE A FILM OR TV ACTOR?

Lisa Rondinelli Albert

Enslow Publishers, Inc.
40 Industrial Road
Box 398
Berkeley Heights, NJ 07922
USA
http://www.enslow.com

Library of Congress Cataloging-in-Publication Data

Albert, Lisa Rondinelli.
    So you want to be a film or TV actor? / Lisa Rondinelli Albert.
       p. cm. — (Careers in film and television)
    Summary: "Details how to become an actor for film and television"—Provided by publisher.
    Includes bibliographical references and index.
    ISBN-13: 978-0-7660-2741-1
    ISBN-10: 0-7660-2741-4
    1. Motion picture acting—Vocational guidance—Juvenile literature. 2. Television acting—
    Vocational guidance—Juvenile literature. I. Title.
    PN1995.9.A26A43 2008
    791.4302'8023—dc22

                                           2007022363

To Our Readers:
We have done our best to make sure all Internet addresses in this book were active and appropriate
when we went to press. However, the author and the publisher have no control over and assume no
liability for the material available on those Internet sites or on other Web sites they may link to. Any
comments or suggestions can be sent by e-mail to comments@enslow.com or to the address on
the back cover.

Oscar®, Academy Awards® and Oscar Night® are all registered trademarks of the
Academy of Motion Picture Arts and Sciences.

Illustration Credits: All images courtesy of Everett Collection, Inc., except p. 95,
courtesy of Jupiterimages Corporation, and p. 100, courtesy of Michael Morgan.

Cover Illustration: Jupiterimages Corporation/ Enslow Publishers, Inc.

CONTENTS

THE EVOLUTION OF ACTING

For anyone who enjoys entertaining and performing, a career as an actor may be the ideal choice. Being a successful actor takes training, skill, and dedication to the craft. It is an exciting and creative profession.

For many people, the word "actor" immediately brings thoughts of fame, fortune, glamour, and Hollywood. But there is a lot more to the business than spotlights and red carpets. Those who truly understand the film and television industry know that achieving success as an actor—as with any career—comes from determination and hard work.

The Screen Actors Guild, the labor union representing working actors, offers this advice to young performers who want to get into acting:

> We call this industry "show business" for a good reason—it is a business. You should treat it as such. That being said, it should also be fun. If for any reason it is not fun and educational for you, get out. If your goal is to make a lot of money and get really famous, really quickly, your hopes will probably never be [realized]. You should be in this business only if you are truly dedicated, have plenty of stamina, and a passion for the craft of acting.[1]

Being an actor requires serious commitment, self-confidence, and the ability to not take rejection personally. There are numerous reasons why an actor may or may not be hired for a part.

THE PLIGHT OF EARLY PERFORMERS

Ancient Greeks and Romans acted onstage and during festivals. Later they were shunned by society with the establishment of the Christianity. Actors then resorted to entertaining as jugglers and jesters as a way to survive and continue performing.[2]

During Medieval times, actors were no longer scorned. Their plays and performances mainly focused on religious themes. During the Renaissance, acting troupes toured Europe and finally earned respect from society. Some actors performing in the plays of William Shakespeare became very well known.

During this period, acting was exclusively done by men and boys in England. As actors, they relied heavily on voice and boisterous movement to covey their characters to live audiences. Women and girls were banned from the stage and any female roles were played by young boys.[3] That changed when King Charles II held the throne. He and his court enjoyed the arts and allowed female actors to perform as well.

Professional actors understand that, sometimes, not getting a part is due to reasons beyond their control.

Back in the 1920s, actors found themselves dealing with a major change in their profession. It was the era of silent films, and actors were accustomed to only using dramatic movements and facial expressions when they performed. Working on silent films meant there was no real need for actors to use their voice. But show business and the movie industry were moving in a new direction. Technology had produced sound recording.

"Wait a minute, wait a minute, you ain't heard nothin' yet!" is the famous line from the first successful sound production on film. It was the voice of Al Jolson, a hardworking vaudeville and Broadway performer who was making his screen-acting debut in the Warner Bros. feature film, *The Jazz Singer*. During the 1927 world premiere of the movie, the audience was stunned to hear the sound of Jolson's voice. Up until this time, movies were silent and dialogue was shown in text for viewers to read. The showing of *The Jazz Singer* at the Tower Theater in Los Angeles, California, soon became the talk of Hollywood.[4]

SILENT FILMS AND TALKIES

With the invention of sound recording, a new era in the film industry was born and Hollywood executives stood up and took notice. The sounds heard in *The Jazz Singer* were made possible by using the Vitaphone—a sound-on-disk system developed by Western Electric and Warner Bros.

The general public embraced the new technology and began to call movies with sound "talkies." All the big studios got in line to use sound in their productions. In 1928, Paramount announced it would only make talkies,[5] even though some studios planned to continue producing silent films.

The entertainment industry was on the cusp of change. It was not long before United Artists, Metro-Goldwyn-Mayer (MGM), and Universal signed on to the new talkies craze. The silent-film era was over. Studio executives instructed their actors to practice talking in front of their bedroom mirrors. Actors now needed to have pleasant voices to go along with their attractive faces. Studios began searching for performers who had both.[6]

The advent of sound brought a whole new dimension to the film industry and it had a direct effect on actors. Some silent-film stars found that their careers came to a halt because of audio technology. Actors who relied only on their physical appearance and movements found themselves out of work. Without voice acting skills, many actors' careers fizzled. Actor John Gilbert was successful in silent movies, but because his voice did not match what his fans expected from such a romantic leading man, his career did not survive the transition to sound.[7]

In order to be cast in a talkie, actors were expected to have clear speaking voices. The ability to use their voices to convey emotion gave some actors an edge. Performers who could control their inflection—a change of pitch or intensity in the voice—rose to the top. Actress Greta Garbo was able to make the transition from silent films to speaking roles even with her thick Swedish accent.[8]

HAROLD LLOYD: COMIC GENIUS OF THE SILENT SCREEN

Actor Harold Lloyd was a comic genius who made his movie debut as an extra in the 1913 film *The Old Monk's Tale*.[9] He was twenty years old and on the brink of stardom. In 1915, his salary for acting in *Just Nuts* was five dollars per day.

EXTRA—Talent used for non-principal roles. Also known as background player.

Lloyd once said "There is something special about the great comedian. He is three-dimensional," and his physical comedy proved it.[10] The daring, dangerous stunts that Lloyd performed in the 1923 movie *Safety Last* made him famous. In the film, Lloyd scales a tall building before gripping the hands of an enormous clock and then dangling in mid-air. To this day, Lloyd's clock scene is regarded as a classic in the movie industry.

Lloyd's career soared throughout the 1920s, and he appeared in dozens of silent films. He had the luxury of financing and controlling his projects, which helped his salary soar. His first sound feature, *Welcome Danger*, cost close to one million dollars to make.[11] It could be said that Harold Lloyd was the Jim Carrey of his time. Fans adored his charm, charisma, and hilarious antics.

In 1927, when the Academy of Motion Picture Arts and Sciences was formed, Lloyd signed on as one of the thirty-six original founders.[12] The year the

Harold Lloyd dangles perilously from the hands of a clock in the silent classic Safety Last **in 1923.**

first talkie was released was also the year Lloyd would begin to see his career evolve.

"Some comedians—in fact most of them—weren't equipped for sound," Lloyd said about transitioning to sound movies. "Now, my going into sound was sort of like when we went into features. It was an evolutionary thing." From a technology standpoint, making the switch from silent films to talkies was difficult for Lloyd.

"It was difficult to keep the same kind of pace in sound pictures as we did in the silents," Lloyd explained.[13] *Welcome Danger* was originally made as a silent film but after Lloyd learned that a low quality sound film was getting attention—even for its cheesy gags—he reacted quickly. Lloyd reworked *Welcome Danger* into a sound film and went on to make seven more sound features.[14]

Lloyd continued to act, but his career in talkies never compared to the success he had found in silent films. His sound movies did not bring in as much money as the studios were used to earning. The studios were faced with difficult decisions during this time of change, and their first concern was box office or ticket sales. It was more practical for them to seek and develop the talent of newcomers and up-and-coming actors than to continue paying such high salaries.

CHARLIE CHAPLIN: THE TRAMP SPEAKS

One actor to make a successful leap from silent films to talkies was Charlie Chaplin. He is best known for his silent role as "The Tramp."

Chaplin's silent-film career began in 1914 with his first silent film, *Making a Living*. In his second picture, *Kid Auto Races at Venice*, Chaplin wore a costume that would become his trademark: baggy pants, a snug jacket, big shoes, a small derby hat, and a cane. A trimmed mustache completed his look, and with that, Chaplin's "Tramp" character was born.[15]

Charlie Chaplin as his classic "Tramp" character.

Chaplin's comic abilities brought scores of fans to watch his silent films. He is credited with boosting the silent-film era from a simple form of entertainment to an art form. Because there was no sound, silent-film stars exaggerated their movements, gestures, and facial expressions in order to entertain. Usually, the pantomiming was full of gags and slapstick humor. Chaplin was its master in his time. Over a twenty-six-year span, he appeared in about seventy short films, movies, and features.[16]

PANTOMIMING—
The act of relaying information or playing scene without the use of one's voice.

With the addition of sound in motion pictures, Chaplin's acting career was at a turning point. At first, he rebelled against the demise of silent films and continued to shoot silent movies even after other studios were making talkies. It was not until 1940 that Chaplin made his talkie debut with the film *The Great Dictator*. The movie was a huge success, and Chaplin proved his acting abilities went beyond the silent screen. Not only was *The Great Dictator* nominated for the Best Picture Academy Award, Chaplin himself received an Oscar nomination in the Best Actor category.

AWARD HISTORY: AND THE OSCAR GOES TO . . .

The very first Academy Awards ceremony was held on May 16, 1929, at the glamorous Hollywood Roosevelt Hotel. During the banquet held in the Blossom Ballroom, the Academy of Motion Picture

Arts and Sciences awarded Chaplin an Oscar for producing, directing, writing, and starring in *The Circus*. The first Oscar statuette ever presented for Best Actor went to Emil Jannings for his roles in *The Last Command* and *The Way of All Flesh*. Warner Bros. also received an award that first year for their groundbreaking production of *The Jazz Singer*.[17]

The youngest actor ever to receive an Oscar was six-year-old Shirley Temple. During the 1934 Academy Awards, Temple was presented with a special Oscar to recognize her contribution to the film industry. This was the time of the Great Depression, and the public whole-heartedly embraced the cheery little star.

Temple was a student at Meglin's Studios, a well-known talent school, and her career began when she was just three years old. With her dimpled cheeks and bouncy curls, she charmed and captivated audiences. Her ability to sing, dance, and act went far beyond her years. In today's terms, Temple would be considered a true Triple Threat— an entertainer who can do it all with ease.

While her movies were not full-blown musical productions, Temple's roles allowed her to sing and dance one or two numbers. One of her most memorable song-and-dance routines was "On the Good Ship Lollipop" in the 1934 film *Bright Eyes*.

Temple joined the ranks of stars who had merchandise fashioned after them. Shirley Temple dolls, records, and clothing brought in millions of dollars.[18] During her amazing career, she appeared in sixty movies between 1932 and 1949, including *The Story of Seabiscuit*.[19] MGM Studios originally wanted Temple to play Dorothy in the 1939 blockbuster, *The Wizard of Oz*, but she was already under contract with Twentieth Century Fox, and the company refused to lend their young star out.

Temple's acting career ended in 1949, when she was in her early twenties. She was honored years later when *Entertainment Weekly* magazine voted her the 38th-Greatest Movie Star of all time. In a 2006 interview, the seventy-seven-year-old Temple offered this advice for today's youth: "Be brave and clear. Follow your heart and don't be overly influenced by outside factors. Be true to yourself."[20]

MUSICALS: FOLLOW THE YELLOW BRICK ROAD TO STARDOM

In 1929, MGM released the musical *Broadway Melody* and advertised it as the first all-talking, all-singing, all-dancing movie. Audiences were impressed. The film, which had taken only twenty-eight days to shoot and $379,000 to produce, brought in a whopping $1.6 million.[21] The success of this first musical was just the beginning for MGM. For actors who could sing and dance, the popularity of musicals was their ticket into the business.

Ten years after the release of *Broadway Melody*, MGM released another blockbuster, *The Wizard of Oz*. Seventeen-year-old Judy Garland became an instant star for her role as Dorothy. Garland had predicted her success many years earlier when, as a young girl, she told a neighbor that she was "going to be a movie star someday."[22]

Prior to starring in *The Wizard of Oz*, Garland had performed with her older sisters, Virginia and Mary Jane. She was six years old in 1928 when the

Bert Lahr, Jack Haley, Ray Bolger, Judy Garland, and Margaret Hamilton in a scene from The Wizard of Oz *(1939).*

sisters joined the Meglin Kiddies, a troupe of child performers from Meglin's Studios. She had traveled with her sisters, performing on radio programs and in front of live audiences. That early experience paid off.

In 1936, Garland was cast in MGM's *Every Sunday* and made three more movies for them before starring in the hugely successful *The Wizard of Oz*. By this time, Garland had read many scripts. Along with each character's lines, shooting scripts contain directions for movements and reactions. In *The Wizard of Oz* script, descriptive setup is placed before any dialogue lines in the following scene:

ELS — The house floating down thru clouds — MLS — Dorothy and Toto lying on bed — the house crashes to ground — Dorothy screams — she looks around — then gets up off the bed — goes to b.g. — picks up the basket — opens door — MCS — Dorothy walks forward — looking around o.s. — CAMERA PANS as she walks to right f.g. — exits — Int. Farm House — MCS — Dorothy enters from l.f.g. and opens the door to reveal Munchkinland — CAMERA BOOMS forward through the door and around to the right — to shoot down on FULL SHOT of Civic Center of the Munchkin Village — Dorothy looks around confused by it all — MLS — Dorothy with Toto in her arms looks about the Village and speaks — Munchkins rise before camera in f.g. and watch her –

DOROTHY (CONT'D)
Toto — I've a feeling we're not in
Kansas anymore.

CS — Dorothy with Toto in her arms
— looks about and speaks —

DOROTHY (CONT'D)
We must be over the rainbow!

LS — Dorothy puts Toto down to the
ground — turns to the b.g. —reacts
and backs slowly toward the camera
— exits right-

LAP DISSOLVE TO:

MLS — Glinda looks o.s. to the right
to Dorothy — MCU — Dorothy look
o.s. to l.f.g. — reacts — speaks —

DOROTHY (CONT'D)
Now I — I know we're not in Kansas.
MLS — Glinda — CAMERA PANS her
right to Dorothy and Toto —

CAMERA TRUCKS forward —
they speak —

GLINDA
Are you a good witch, or a bad witch?

DOROTHY
Who, me? Why, I'm not a witch at all.
I'm Dorothy Gale from Kansas.[23]

After the huge success of *The Wizard of Oz*, scripts poured in for Garland. By 1950, she had starred in ten movies and had become a household name. Around this time, plans were in the works for another MGM musical, *Singin' in the Rain*.

When *Singin' in the Rain* was released in 1952, Garland was thirty years old and her career was still going strong. In 1955, she was awarded a Golden Globe for Best Motion Picture Actress for her performance in *A Star is Born* (1954). The musical drama was also nominated for Oscars in six categories during the Academy Awards, including a nomination for Best Actress in a Leading Role. [24]

Even though Garland performed the song "Singin' in the Rain" in the 1940 film *Little Nellie Kelly*, [25] it was Debbie Reynolds—a nineteen-year-old newcomer—who was cast in the role of Kathy Selden in the 1952 film, *Singin' in the Rain*. Reynolds did not have extensive dancing experience and worked hard to learn the routines. Years after filming the movie, she commented that making *Singin' in the Rain* and childbirth were two of the hardest things she had ever had to do. Just to get to the studio, Reynolds had to wake up at four o'clock in the morning and take three buses to arrive on time.

In *Singin' in the Rain*, Reynolds was paired up with the very popular Gene Kelly, who played her leading man, Don Lockwood. The humorous story line follows two silent-film stars and reveals how their careers were affected by the invention of sound.

Debbie Reynolds and Gene Kelly in a promotional photo for Singin' in the Rain.

While Don Lockwood's smooth voice allows him to make the transition without a problem, his silent-film leading lady, Lina Lamont (played by Jean Hagen), finds it much more difficult. Her horrible, screechy voice is then dubbed by Debbie Reynolds' character, Kathy Selden.

The voice-over dubbing is revealed during a humorous scene. Lina Lamont lip-synchs in front of a live audience while Kathy Selden sings behind a curtain. When Don Lockwood and his partner raise the curtain, the secret is revealed and Kathy finally gets credit for her acting and voice.

Reynolds found success playing girl-next-door comedic roles and was given the Lifetime Achievement Award in Comedy at the 1997 American Comedy Awards.[26] In 2006, the American Film Institute named *Singin' in the Rain* the number one musical in American film history.

Since their inception, on-screen musicals have catapulted the careers of many actors and continue to do so. The following is just a sampling of actors who have sung and danced their way to success in musicals:

Julie Andrews:
Mary Poppins in *Mary Poppins* (1964)
Maria in *The Sound of Music* (1965)
Victoria in *Victor/Victoria* (1982)
Queen Clarisse Renaldi in *The Princess Diaries* (2001) and *The Princess Diaries 2: Royal Engagement* (2004)

Olivia Newton-John:
Sandy Olsson in *Grease* (1978)

Vanessa Anne Hudgens:
Gabriella Montez in *High School Musical* (2006) and
High School Musical 2: Sing It All or Nothing! (2007)

Zac Efron:
Troy Bolton in *High School Musical* (2006) and *High School Musical 2: Sing It All or Nothing!* (2007)
Link Larkin in *Hairspray* (2007)

THE OSCAR

An MGM art director, Cedric Gibbons, designed the trophy, but George Stanley, a Los Angeles sculptor, created the actual Oscar statuette. It depicts a knight holding a sword while standing on a reel of film.[27]

Early on, the trophy was made of solid bronze and simply called the "Academy Award of Merit." But after the Academy librarian, Margaret Herrick, mentioned that the statue resembled her Uncle Oscar, the nickname spread amongst Academy staff. It was not until 1939 that the Academy itself began to refer to the statue as Oscar.

Today's Oscar is cast using the metal alloy, britannium. Once it is gold-plated, the thirteen-and-a-half-inch statuette weighs a hefty eight and a half pounds.

POITIER PAVED THE WAY

One of the most respected actors to be awarded an Oscar is Sidney Poitier. Growing up in the Bahamas and coming to the United States at the age of fifteen, Poitier faced several challenges. A documentary produced by American Masters describes how Poitier settled in New York and worked as a dishwasher and later exchanged janitor duties for acting lessons. Part of Poitier's charm is his slight Caribbean accent, which he tried to erase completely by listening to American radio.[28]

In 1946, Poitier made his Broadway acting debut and worked his way up to his first movie, *No Way Out*, in 1950. In the fifties, Poitier had gained popularity and was being offered a steady stream of movie roles. All of the years he had spent studying at the American Negro Theater had paid off.

The 1950s were a time when society struggled with race relations, and Poitier, along with several other prominent actors of color, helped bridge a racial gap by portraying characters that everyone could relate to. In 1964, Poitier was awarded the Best Actor Oscar for his role in the 1963's *Lilies of the Field*. It was a groundbreaking moment because Poitier was the first black actor to achieve such a well-deserved honor.

Poitier had become a hero to many, but in particular, to other African Americans. After he received his award, Poitier commented to the *New York Times*, "I'd like to think it will help someone, but I

Sidney Poitier in **They Call Me Mister Tibbs!** *(1970).*

don't believe my Oscar will be a sort of magic wand that will wipe away the restrictions on job opportunities for Negro actors."[29]

Poitier's humble attitude and fine acting ability have made him a role model and legend of his time. Between 1950 and 1997, Poitier acted in or directed more than fifty movies and earned dozens of awards. Many credit him with paving the way for

SALARIES OF THE STARS

Harold Lloyd:
Just Nuts (1915): $5 per day
Professor Beware (1938): $125,000
The Sin of Harold Diddlebock (1947): $140,000

Shirley Temple:
The Red-Haired Alibi (1932): $50 for two days
Stand Up and Cheer! (1934): $75 per week
Since You Went Away (1944): $2,200 per week
Fort Apache (1948): $110,000

Judy Garland:
Every Sunday (1936): $100 per week
The Wizard of Oz (1939): $500 per week
The Harvey Girls (1946): $3,000 per week
A Star is Born (1954): $100,000 plus 50 percent
of profits

other talented Oscar winners such as Denzel Washington, Halle Barry, and Jamie Foxx.[30]

In 2002, Poitier was given an Honorary Oscar from the Academy recognizing his extraordinary performances and unique presence on the screen and for representing the industry with dignity, style, and intelligence.

PIONEERS OF THE CRAFT

Long before silent films, musicals, and movies were popular, the ancient Greeks performed tragedy and comedy onstage. Similar to today's dramas, a tragedy's plot focused on one main character throughout the story.[1] The Greek philosopher Aristotle described the elements of tragedy this way: "Every Tragedy, therefore, must have six parts, which parts determine its quality—namely, Plot, Character, Diction, Thought, Spectacle, Song."[2]

Early comedy was not as plot- or character-driven as tragedy, but it did offer its own level of entertainment. Similar to comedic actors of today, the goal of ancient performers was to be funny and make their audiences laugh.

It has been said that the Greek poet Thespis invented tragedy. On top of that, some credit him with introducing the prologue—a stage technique used at the beginning of a performance to set up the story line for the audience.

Actors of these early times began to be referred to as Thespians, a term which continues to be used to describe someone in the drama field. Thespians often used masks to convey emotions to their live audiences. Even though the facts are sketchy, Thespis has been credited as being the first to use masks onstage.[3] To this day, many acting organizations, including the Screen Actors Guild (SAG), use the tragedy/comedy masks—also known as the happy/sad masks—as their logo.

GREAT INFLUENCES OF THE ART FORM

One of the most influential actors of the twentieth century was Konstantin Stanislavky. As a member of Russia's Moscow Art Theater, Stanislavky developed a system which made acting a higher art form. His system led actors to use "emotional memory" when preparing for a role. Prior to his system, actors did not use emotion as a tool; instead, they simply tried to become their characters.

Using Stanislavky's "system," actors were encouraged to draw upon their emotions in order to give more realistic performances. Actors were taught to recollect feelings from their personal experiences as a way to express what their character might be feeling. If an actor was playing a character who was afraid, that actor needed to remember a frightening event from his or her own experiences.[4]

Stanislavky gave this advice to aspiring performers: "Young actors, fear your admirers! Learn in time, from your first steps, to hear, understand and love the cruel truth about yourselves. Find out who can tell you that truth and talk of your art only with those who can tell you the truth."[5]

LEE STRASBERG AND "THE METHOD"

After spending years studying the Stanislavky system in America, Lee Strasberg became one of the founding members of an American acting company, Group Theater. Noted as the first company in America to perform as an ensemble, Group Theater began operation in 1931 and dissolved in 1941.[6]

ENSEMBLE—A group of performers whose roles are equally important.

Several of the original founders of Group Theater reorganized in 1947 and opened the Actors Studio. Strasberg joined the Actors Studio in 1949 and was appointed artistic director in 1951.[7]

During his years at the Actors Studio, Strasberg used the Stanislavsky system as a springboard for developing what is now known as "The Method." He refined the system and added his own techniques and acting exercises. This updated form of method acting concentrated on relaxation, sensory memory, improvisation, and transformation.[8]

IMPROVISATION— To act or perform without any preparation.

Lee Strasberg in a scene from Going In Style *(1979)*

In a 1975 lecture in front of a group of his students, Strasberg explained the primary purpose of Actors Studio:

> To demonstrate that there is such a thing as a technique of acting. That there is such a thing as a procedure in acting. That these procedures are not individually conditioned, but that they relate to *all* actors, and to the problems that *all* actors experience. And these procedures are the end result of a long process of search, of investigation, of observation . . . mainly contributed to by Stanislavsky, but by other actors in the past that have found their way towards it without knowing what they had found. And Stanislavsky somehow, becoming aware of what they had found, built it into something called "the Stanislavsky System," the actual meaning of which many people, even in Russia, misunderstand and are confused by, and which "the method" based itself on, and in turn took up, added to. And frankly, I believe quite honestly, made it into an international base for actors' work.[9]

Strasberg continued his lecture and compared "The Method" to common terms used in the visual arts:

> The "method" is a word that is now widely used. That's the first time in the theatre that anything like that has happened. In the other arts, you use the word "cubist," "abstract art," "modern art," and so on and so forth. These words become general

knowledge and are often used. Not in a simple technical understanding of what they involve, but become words in general usage. Never had that been true in the theatre. The first time that that was true was as a result of 'the method', that brought into language and to people's awareness somehow something called "*the* method".[10]

Strasberg died in 1982, but the Actors Studio continues to teach and develop talented performers. Many famous actors studied at the Actors Studio during the years it was guided by Strasberg. Some of his most successful students include Paul Newman, Al Pacino, Dustin Hoffman, and Marilyn Monroe. Strasberg's advice to his students was simply, "Try not to act, be yourself, use gestures in a manner that you use in private life."[11]

MARILYN MONROE

In the span of Marilyn Monroe's short life of thirty-six years, she went from orphan to superstar. She began her career in the public eye as a swimsuit model in the late 1940s. Over the course of her career, Monroe made movies for Twentieth Century Fox, MGM, Columbia, and United Artists.[12] Even though she was not deemed a great theatrical actress, Monroe became known as a performer with a comic style all her own.

She was often cast as a ditzy blonde bombshell, but she yearned for more serious parts. She once stated that she did not care about money. She just

Marilyn Monroe performs in the main production number from Gentlemen Prefer Blondes.

wanted to be wonderful. She explained further by saying, "I want to be a real actress instead of a superficial one. For the first time, I'm learning to use myself fully as an actress. I want to add something to what I had before. I want to be in the kind of pictures where I can develop."[13]

Monroe's acting talent was recognized in 1957 when she was nominated for a Golden Globe for her portrayal of Cherie in the musical comedy *Bus Stop*.

By the time *Some Like It Hot* was released in 1959, Monroe had improved her skills enough to go on to win the Golden Globe for Best Motion Picture Actress in 1960. She began at the bottom in terms of earnings, but was very highly paid by the end of her career:

Scudda Hoo! Scudda Hay! (1948): $75 per week

The Asphalt Jungle (1950): $1,050

All About Eve (1950): $500 per week, 1-week guarantee

Gentlemen Prefer Blondes (1953): $1,250 per week

There's No Business Like Show Business (1954): $1,000 per week

The Seven Year Itch (1955): $1,500 per week

Some Like It Hot (1959): $200,000 plus 10 percent gross over $4 million.

The Misfits (1961): $250,000

DUSTIN HOFFMAN

Dustin Hoffman studied acting at the Pasadena Playhouse before he went to New York to train with Lee Strasberg. He acted in college productions, but the buzz about his talent began after he landed roles in off-Broadway productions. Hollywood noticed Hoffman's stage presence and he was cast as Benjamin Braddock in the 1967 movie *The Graduate.*[14]

He was thirty-one years old when he began his film career. Even among the classically handsome or veteran actors, Hoffman stood out for his acting depth and skill. Jane Jenkins, a well-respected casting director and longtime friend of Hoffman, recounted his early days in her book, *A Star is Found*: "Back in 1963, he was just a talented guy with a big nose. The ethnic look was not yet in, and 'Dusty' was struggling—even though we all knew that he was far and away the best actor in our little company."[15]

Hoffman's studying paid off and he was rewarded at the 1968 Golden Globe Awards where he accepted the award for Most Promising Newcomer. That award would account for just one of more than seventy awards he has won or been nominated for.

The fact that Hoffman did not fit the typical good-looking leading man mold allowed him to break the stereotypical pattern of what audiences had come to expect in a lead actor. Jenkins describes actors like Hoffman as "straight-out character actors, even when they're playing the biggest part in the movie."[16]

Hoffman is known for his ability to take on a wide range of roles. In the 1970 film *Little Big Man*, Hoffman's character, Jack Crabb, ages from seventeen to one-hundred-twenty-one years old. On top of the movie's success, Hoffman earned an entry in *The Guinness Book of World Records* for "Greatest Age Span Portrayed By A Movie Actor."

In 1982, Hoffman starred in *Tootsie*, a movie that continues to be viewed as one of his best comic roles. Hoffman plays Michael Dorsey, an unemployed actor who masquerades as a woman in order to land acting jobs. The comic twist comes when his alter ego, Dorothy Michaels, becomes a popular soap opera actress.

Over the span of his career, Hoffman has been recognized with dozens of nominations and awards. His performance in *Tootsie* received critical acclaim from fans and reviews alike. Hoffman received an Oscar nomination for Best Actor in a Leading Role and a Golden Globe award for his work in *Tootsie*.

Seven years later, in 1989, Hoffman was again nominated for an Oscar for Best Actor in a Leading Role. This time around, Hoffman was up for the award for his believable and stunning portrayal of Raymond Babbitt, a mentally disabled man in *Rain Man* (1988). Not surprisingly, Hoffman took home the Oscar.

Hoffman showcased his great comedic timing and this versatility in the 1991 adventure-comedy *Hook*, where he wore a mustache and long black wig for his role as Captain Hook. This role broadened Hoffman's audience to include young viewers. Young audiences might recognize his voice as well. He has played the part of several animated characters. His voice-over performances include Tucker in *Racing Stripes* (2005), Shifu in *Kung Fu Panda* (2008), and Roscuro, the rat, in *The Tale of Despereaux* (2008).

Remembering the years he struggled to make a living as a working actor, Hoffman said, "I lived below the official American poverty line until I was 31."[17] His hard work, determination, and skills have allowed

Dustin Hoffman showed his versatility as an actor when he portrayed a man portraying a woman in Tootsie.

Hoffman to remain one of Hollywood's most sought after actors. This is evidenced by his growing pay scale over the course of his career:

The Graduate (1967): $17,000

Midnight Cowboy (1969): $250,000

John and Mary (1969): $425,000

Papillon (1973): $1,250,000

Rain Man (1988): $5,800,000 plus a percentage of the gross

STELLA ADLER: BORN INTO THE BUSINESS

Both of Stella Adler's parents were actors, so it is not surprising that she, too, found success in the industry. During her early acting career, she traveled and performed throughout Europe, South America, and the United States. Her vaudeville performances brought her acclaim, but she yearned for greater opportunities and roles that would bring her more recognition.

Adler became a member of Group Theater in 1931, the same year she met her husband, Harold Clurman—one of the group's founders. She left the group to study under Konstantin Stanislavsky and returned in 1934 with a new perspective on the craft.

Adler spent three more years acting with the group before leaving for Hollywood in 1937. She appeared in several movies and then returned to Broadway to act and direct. She became recognized as a leader in the industry and, in 1949, she opened what is known today as the Stella Adler Conservatory of Acting.

"You act with your soul," Adler is quoted telling her students. "That's why you all want to be actors, because your souls are not used up by life."[18] Her teaching and guidance produced some extremely well-known actors, including Marlon Brando and Robert De Niro.

The success of the Stella Adler Conservatory was not diminished after Adler's death in 1992. It continues to be a steady training ground for aspiring actors. Alumni include:

Genevieve Cortese—*Wildfire*, television series (29 episodes, 2005–2007)

Sarah Utterback—*Medium*, television series (2 episodes, 2005), *Grey's Anatomy* (15 episodes, 2005–2007)

Mark Ruffalo—*13 Going on 30* (2004), *Collateral* (2004), *Zodiac* (2007)

MODERN DEVELOPMENTS

When the Screen Actors Guild (SAG) was established in 1933, it created the largest labor union for actors. The formation of SAG was a triumph for actors who had been subject to unfair working conditions. According to the SAG Web site, nearly 120,000 working actors are represented by the union.

Membership in SAG should come after an actor has earned experience elsewhere. Actors who are ready to join SAG have usually spent time acting in small projects and onstage. Joining the organization is considered a milestone in an acting career, but it is not something that should be rushed into.

SAG advises actors, "don't be in a hurry to join SAG. Make sure you are ready to compete as a professional. Prepare yourself by studying, performing in plays and non-union on-camera projects in order to build your resume and gain valuable experience. When you are offered your

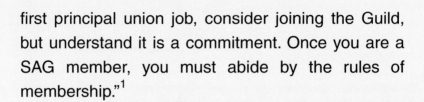

first principal union job, consider joining the Guild, but understand it is a commitment. Once you are a SAG member, you must abide by the rules of membership."[1]

DAKOTA FANNING

Many actors begin their careers by performing in small productions at schools or community theaters. Actor Dakota Fanning's career began at a playhouse where children performed plays for small audiences. Fanning's talent was obvious, not only to her parents, but to those who ran the playhouse.

After looking into acting options for their daughter, Fanning's parents were advised to move to Los Angeles. The plan was to move from their Georgia home for a six-week period and try to find work for Dakota. After Fanning was cast in a national commercial for Tide laundry detergent, the family decided to turn their temporary move into a permanent one.[2]

By 2000 and 2001, Fanning had been cast to play several roles on various popular television series such as *ER* and *Malcolm in the Middle*. She worked her way up, and when opportunity presented itself, she auditioned to play the part of Lucy Diamond Dawson in the 2001 film *I Am Sam*. Fanning won the role and her performance was that of a seasoned professional.

In 2002, members of the Screen Actors Guild recognized Fanning's efforts. She was eight years

Dakota Fanning takes directions from director Gary Winick on the set of Charlotte's Web *in 2006.*

old when her acting peers nominated her to receive the award of Outstanding Performance by a Female Actor in a Supporting Role. She was the youngest person to ever be nominated for a Screen Actors Guild award. Four years and nine films later, Fanning won the Saturn Award given by the Academy of Science Fiction, Fantasy and Horror Films. Her role as Rachel Ferrier in *War of the Worlds* earned her Best Performance by a Younger Actor.

Fanning was reportedly earning $3 million per movie in 2005 and offers continued to pour in.[3] In

2006, she played Fern in the family film *Charlotte's Web,* and in the 2008 animated movie *Coraline*, she is the voice of Coraline.

"I've always wanted to be an actress, ever since I was a little girl," Fanning has said. As a little girl, her pretending consisted of her playing the role of the mom while her sister played the daughter role. Speaking of her early acting at home she confessed, "I wanted to be an actress on television and movies instead of just around the house."[4] At a very young age, Fanning's dreams have all come true.

MAKING A BIG SPLASH

Some of the most successful actors began their careers by immersing themselves in community theaters or school drama clubs. Becoming involved in local programs is an excellent way to get a feel for acting and gain experience.

Actor Tom Hanks got his start while he was a student at Skyline High School in Oakland, California. After Hanks' drama teacher encouraged him to pursue acting, he spent a lot of time on and around the stage. He did not limit his study of the stage to just acting; he also learned the behind-the-scenes jobs.[5] After high school, Hanks worked his way up to acting on stages in New York and Los Angeles.

Hanks' knack for comedic roles led him to be cast in a starring role for the ABC-TV sitcom *Bosom Buddies* in 1980. In this silly series, Hanks played

Kip Wilson, a character who disguised himself as a woman in order to live in an inexpensive, all-female apartment building. The series lasted only two years but in 1982 Hanks made an appearance on *Happy Days,* where he met Ron Howard on the set.

Although he had previously played Richie on *Happy Days*, Howard was then directing the movie *Splash*. He asked Hanks to audition for a secondary role, but after Hanks read, he was awarded the lead. *Splash* hit the theaters in 1984.[6]

Tom Hanks and Daryl Hannah in a scene from Splash *(1984)*

Hanks went on to make seven more movies before landing the leading role in the movie *Big*. In *Big*, Hanks plays Josh, a twelve-year-old boy who becomes trapped in a grown man's body after wishing to be big. This role earned Hanks an Oscar nomination for Best Actor in a Leading Role. The nominations and awards Hanks received for *Big* kept coming in. He won a Golden Globe for Best Performance by an Actor in a Motion Picture (Comedy/Musical) in addition to claiming the top prize of Funniest Actor in a Motion Picture at the American Comedy Awards.[7]

After Hanks' blockbuster success in *Big*, he made eight more films before winning both an Oscar and a Golden Globe for his portrayal of a lawyer afflicted with AIDS in the 1993 drama *Philadelphia*. Hanks' ability to take on serious roles was cemented with these awards. The very next year, the movie industry buzzed when Hanks swept the top awards again. He received an Oscar, a Golden Globe, and a Screen Actors Guild award for his 1994 portrayal of a mentally challenged man in *Forrest Gump*.

Hanks' versatile ability to take on comedic or dramatic roles allowed him the freedom to choose a variety of parts. In the animated movies *Toy Story* (1995) and *Toy Story 2* (1999), Hanks voiced the toy cowboy, Woody. In 2004, Hanks returned to animated films by portraying several characters in the movie *The Polar Express*. He can also be heard as Woody Car in the 2006 animated movie *Cars*.

Beginning with his television career, Hanks has worked with some of the top directors and producers in the industry, including Steven Spielberg and Penny Marshall. Ron Howard and Hanks have worked on several films together and in 2006 they teamed up again for the multi-million-dollar hit *The Da Vinci Code*.

Some actors who achieve success acting in multi-million-dollar movies end up making the transition into producing movies as well. Along with a dozen or more films in various stages of production, Hanks is one of the producers of *Where The Wild Things Are*. The film, due out in 2008, is an adaptation of the classic children's book by Maurice Sendak.

Even though starting an acting career on television, as Hanks did, may not always lead to Hollywood fame and multi-million-dollar deals, it does provide a lot of opportunities for new and veteran actors. Some television actors are content to work on series or soap operas, although many aspire to leap over to the big screen. The ladder of success in the business can be a tall one. It is up to the individual actor to pursue the level they are comfortable with. Of course, hard work, timing, casting directors, agents, and a bit of luck all play a part in attaining goals.

THE EFFECT OF TELEVISION

The invention of television certainly increased the availability of work for actors. In 1947, puppet shows, such as *The Howdy Doody Show*, were popular programs for children and westerns were watched by all ages. Hopalong Cassidy, Roy Rogers, and Gene Autry—known as "The Singing Cowboy"—became household names.[8]

By 1952, the rising need for talent to work on television brought about a new and improved union. That year, two separate unions—the American Federation of Radio Artists (AFRA) and Television Authority (TVA)—merged to establish the American Federation of Television and Radio Artists (AFTRA).[9] According to its Web site, AFTRA is a national labor union representing more than 70,000 performers, journalists, and other artists working in the entertainment and news media.[10]

Television rapidly gained popularity. By the early 1950s more than 21 million sets were in use. In 1952, the first serialized daytime drama debuted to TV viewers. *The Guiding Light*, which began on the radio in 1927, moved to CBS-TV. The show began as a 15-minute daily program. Over the years, its time slot grew to an hour and its title was eventually changed to simply *Guiding Light*. Today, daytime dramas—now known as soap operas—provide actors with regular work. In the entertainment business, regular work also means a steady income.

While many actors aspire to work on soap operas and are content to remain as long as their characters have storylines, the daytime dramas have acted as career stepping-stones for some actors. The exposure actors get while working on soap operas can help them land roles on primetime television shows, cable programs, or the big screen.

ACTORS IN DAYTIME DRAMAS

Courtney Cox of *Friends*, *Scream*, and *Dirt* fame began her career in 1984 as Bunny on *As the World Turns*. She worked on various television series, movies, and sitcoms before 1994 when she signed on to play Monica Geller on *Friends*.

Hayden Panettiere had a small part on *One Life to Live* before playing Elizabeth "Lizzie" Spaulding on *Guiding Light*. Before landing her role as Claire Bennet on *Heroes*, she appeared on several sitcoms, series, and movies.

Sarah Michelle Gellar had a recurring role on *All My Children* and appeared on other series before being hired to play Buffy Summers on *Buffy the Vampire Slayer* in 1997. Her big screen roles include *I Know What You Did Last Summer* (1997) and *The Grudge* (2004).

John Stamos began his career in 1982 as Blackie on *General Hospital* and acted in many series and TV movies before taking the role of Jesse on *Full House* from 1987 through 1995. He continued making movies and television appearances and, in 2005, he was signed to play Dr. Tony Gates on the long-running primetime medical drama *ER*.

Throughout the 1950s, television programming boomed. Even shows that began as radio programs were finding their way onto the small screen. *Gunsmoke* was a longtime radio program before it debuted as a television series in 1955.[11] By this time, home audiences were glued to their sets watching comedies, dramas, game shows, and variety programs. The availability of work for television actors expanded to movies by the mid-1960s.

Hayden Panettiere as Claire, the indestructible cheerleader in Heroes.

In 1964, *See How They Run* was billed as the first "made-for-TV" movie when it was broadcast on NBC.[12]

Eight years after the first TV movie debuted, Home Box Office (HBO) officially began on cable television. HBO was the first pay-TV network available to home viewers. The film and television industry saw an opportunity for enormous growth and by the end of the 1970s, close to 16 million households subscribed to cable.[13] By 1987—fifteen years after HBO premiered—more than half the homes in the United States received cable. As of 2005, an estimated 79 percent of households had two or more televisions. Even though not all of them were available to the average consumer, there were more than 1,300 cable channels.[14]

The popularity and growth of cable television created a broad range of opportunities for actors. Networks such as Nickelodeon and the Disney Channel continue to develop on-screen personalities through original series and movies. The huge success of Disney Channel's 2006 movie *High School Musical* made Vanessa Anne Hudgens, Zac Efron, and Corbin Bleu household names. Although each of them had prior TV, film, or theater credits, their roles in *High School Musical* really thrust them into the limelight.

Vanessa Anne Hudgens' first television gig was a commercial. She had auditioned in place of a friend who was not able to go and ended up getting cast.

Since 2002, Hudgens' appearances on several television shows include a recurring role as Corrie on *The Suite Life of Zack and Cody*. Her big screen credits include the R-rated movie *Thirteen* (2003) and PG-rated *Thunderbirds* (2004).[15]

Before her starring role as Gabriella Montez in *High School Musical*, Hudgens performed in theater musicals such as *The Wizard of Oz*, *Evita*, *The Little Mermaid*, and many more. Speaking of her favorite musicals, Hudgens told *People* magazine, "I really like *Grease*, *The Sound of Music*, and *Bye Bye Birdie*. And *West Side Story*. I want to play Maria. That's my dream job. I hope a studio will hear that."[16]

Both Zac Efron and Corbin Bleu began their careers onstage. After taking singing lessons, Efron landed roles in several productions including *Peter Pan*, *Little Shop of Horrors*, and *Gypsy*, which ran for ninety shows. By 2002, he had worked on several series before landing the part of Cameron Bale on *Summerland* in 2005.

Like Hudgens, Efron also appeared on Disney Channel's *The Suite Life of Zack and Cody*. Along with his leading role as Troy Bolton in *High School Musical*, Efron's prior experience onstage opened more doors for him. In the 2007 movie version of the Broadway hit, *Hairspray*, Efron plays Link Larkin, the cute and popular boyfriend character.[17]

Corbin Bleu was a two-year-old toddler when he began landing jobs on commercials. He appeared in spots for Life cereal, Nabisco, and Hasbro.

Monique Coleman, Corbin Bleu, Vanessa Anne Hudgens, Zac Efron, Ashley Tisdale, and Lucas Grabeel perform "What Time Is It" in High School Musical 2 *(2007).*

Actors' Unions: The Four A's

While joining a union is not necessary for actors who perform in high school plays, drama clubs, or college performances, becoming a member is something an actor should consider once offered work under contract. Along with the Screen Actors Guild (SAG), there are four other unions that represent entertainers.

Actors Equity Association (AEA) is made up primarily of theater and stage performers. The AEA membership booklet describes the organization: "We are the union that supports, promotes and fosters the art of professional theatre. Our members can be found performing in all kinds of theatrical venues: on Broadway, in respected regional theatres, in Disney World and in small professional theatres throughout the United States. We are the union that protects artists while they practice their craft . . . their profession."[18]

AFTRA, the American Federation of Television and Radio Actors, represents actors and performers who work on TV, digital media, and radio.

The American Guild of Musical Artists (AGMA) is an organization for dance, concert, and opera performers.

Performers working in nightclubs, arena shows, and ice shows have a union of their own as well. They are covered by the American Guild of Variety Artists (AGVA).

While each union is independently operated, they make up a group of sister unions that support one another's efforts in representing workers. Together, these five unions make up the Associated Actors and Artists of America—the four A's.

When he was a little older, Bleu took jazz and ballet lessons in addition to pursue modeling. He was only six years old when he was cast in his first professional acting job in an off-Broadway play.

After his family moved from New York to Los Angeles in 1996, seven-year-old Bleu was cast in several small roles on television and in feature films. He continued to hone his acting skills while attending the Debbie Allen Dance Academy. Bleu was a freshman at Los Angeles County High School for the Arts when he was cast in his first leading role as Austin in the Twentieth Century Fox movie *Catch That Kid* (2004).[19]

High School Musical was a phenomenal hit with audiences ranging in age from six to fourteen years. Its television premiere had a record-setting 7.7 million viewers, and it was the top-rated movie during its first month of repeat showings.[20] The cast of *High School Musical*, including Hudgens, Efron, and Bleu, reunited in the 2007 sequel, *High School Musical 2: Sing It All or Nothing!* For each of these three actors, gaining experience early on by working onstage served them well.

4

SHOW BUSINESS:
WHAT IT TAKES TO BE A
WORKING ACTOR

To succeed as an actor there must be a clear understanding that first—and foremost—it is an occupation. The driving factor to enter the field must be a desire to perform and not lofty dreams of fame and fortune. It is an exciting and rewarding business for those who are willing to work in order to reach their dreams.

Natural talent, determination, self-assurance, and willingness to learn are all good characteristics to have while pursuing a career as an actor. Actors who know their strengths and have an idea of what types of roles they can fill have a healthy outlook compared to actors who believe they can do it all.

Actor Raven-Symoné Pearman, also known simply as Raven, has a knack for playing female characters who are easy to relate to. Even though she began in the business as a toddler,

Raven kept setting goals for herself. "When I was younger, I just had the typical 'kid roles,' and now I'm actually getting to do character roles and different people on *That's So Raven*," she said, speaking of her acting growth.[1]

DOING YOUR HOMEWORK

The goal of becoming an actor can be realized when practical steps are taken. Enroll in drama clubs, take acting classes, or study one-on-one with a reputable acting coach. Regardless of where actors receive their education, training of some sort is highly recommended. Most educational programs and workshops focus on specific training. Auditioning, cold reading, scene-study, film acting, and improvisational exercises are samples of the types of classes actors need to take.[2]

Talent can be developed and enriched by learning how to use voice, movement, and emotion. Lee Strasberg defined acting this way: "Acting is to live onstage. This means an actor must be able to react to an imaginary stimulus just as hard as he would to a real stimulus."[3]

The Method, taught by Strasberg, consists of various vocal, physical, and emotional exercises. During the exercises, Strasberg would determine a student's acting potential. He explained by using this example: "Suppose I hit you in the face. You will either pull back, look angry, look sad, rub your cheek, perhaps shout at me or strike me. You had an

Raven-Symoné Pearman got her big break at a very young age when she first appeared on The Cosby Show. *Today, she is best known for her self-titled show* That's So Raven.

honest reaction. I didn't have to tell you what to do or feel. Now the true actor, he will react just as honestly even if I pretend to slap him. A beautiful voice and good looks—no, this doesn't make the actor. Can he react? Well, that is the question."[4]

Even actors who have extensive training or schooling are not guaranteed to make it in the business. Those who go above and beyond the classroom and immerse themselves in everything acting-related are generally the ones who get noticed. Along with learning the craft, reading books about acting, going to plays and studying movies are important too. Even though these pursuits would not generally be listed on an actor's résumé, doing those things will nurture talent and create a better understanding and respect for the job.

Putting together a résumé and head shot package is a must for actors. A head shot is an 8″ x 10″ photograph showing only the head and shoulders. A resume is a summary of an actor's experience. Resumes are usually trimmed to the size of the head shot and the two are stapled together. Any acting credits, including school plays or community theaters, are listed. Until an actor achieves these types of credits, the résumé focuses on special training, schooling, and other educational programs.

Basic physical information such as height, weight, dress or coat size, and hair and eye color are noted as well. It is also a good idea to highlight other skills. Whether it be juggling, scuba diving, yodeling or whatever, do not be shy. Be honest. A casting director or talent agent may make a favorable decision based on these additional skills.[5]

Additional items to list include any union memberships and current contact information. Because resumes may be passed around from person to person, industry professionals warn against including private phone numbers and home addresses. It is best to include alternate phone numbers such as an answering service, cell phone, or pager if available. Of course, once an actor has a talent agent, that contact information is provided. Most resumes also do not include an actor's age. The reason behind this omission is that actors who are twenty years old may be able to play older or younger characters, depending on their appearance and their abilities.[6]

A growing trend in the industry includes the use of the Internet, Web sites and e-mail as communication tools for the audition and casting process. Many production companies and agencies accept resumes and photograph via e-mail. Even so, it is strongly recommended that actors use good judgment when sending any personal information or photograph over the Internet. Safe and harmless— and even flattering—as it may be to get a request for a resume package, be certain the requesting party is legitimate. It is also a good idea to set up a separate e-mail account for correspondence and keep personal information on Web sites to a minimum.

The Web sites of Actors' Equity Association (AEA) and Screen Actors Guild Independent (SAGINDIE) offer enhanced tools which allow actors to view postings of upcoming auditions around the country. Breakdowns and contact information are also provided. Most companies instruct potential actors to send resumes and head shots to a listed e-mail address. Resume packages sent over the Internet should be as professional as any that would be sent via the postal service.

Some actors promote themselves by having a Web site to showcase their resume, head shots, e-mail address, and contact information (such as an agent or post office box). There may be instances when an actor may find it more practical to simply direct a potential employer to a Web site. Keeping the Web site information up-to-date is important. Photographs that are years old or using out of date material could wind up costing an actor a job.

GETTING TO KNOW CASTING DIRECTORS

It is not uncommon for actors to send resume packages to talent agents and casting directors at the same time. Casting directors are in charge of finding actors to fill roles. They may be part of a production crew or an independent casting director. Regardless of their status—whether a crewmember or freelance—the casting director plays a large role in an actor's career. Since they are hired to work for the companies that make films, movies, and commercials, casting directors comb through hundreds of resumes and head shots to find the right actor.

Once a casting director receives a script, their task is to find just the right actor for each character. Usually, the first step is contacting talent agents with whom they have working relationships to discuss available clients. This is one reason having a talent agent is a good career move for actors. Actors who are represented by talent agencies are generally considered for auditions before actors who are not with a talent agency.

After making contacts through agencies, the casting director will broaden their search by sending out what is called a breakdown—a detailed listing of the types of roles to be cast, including speaking and non-speaking roles. These listings are available to talent agents and agencies all over the world as long as they subscribe to the service.[7] Talent agents will read through the breakdown, match their clients to a listing, and arrange auditions.

Whether or not an actor has a talent agent, the main goal should always be getting an audition. Auditioning can be time-consuming and tiring work. Open casting calls—often referred to as cattle calls—attract hordes of hopeful actors. One disadvantage of the open casting call is the fierce competition. Plus, there is no guarantee the time spent will lead to a role, even a minor one. Even so, cattle calls do have their advantages.

Much like the auditions seen on *American Idol*, actors are given a short amount of time in front of the casting director. The unprepared actors and people with little or no talent are weeded out quickly. This is a good thing for actors who know what they are doing. When attending an open casting call, be prepared to wait in line for several hours and make the best impression possible.[8]

CASTING AUDITIONS AND THE CALLBACK

It is not uncommon for actors to go on dozens of auditions before being asked for a callback or landing a role. Persistence is key, and each audition should be a learning experience. Cattle call auditions can be great for exposure even when an actor does not get cast. Sometimes, during cattle calls, the casting director may be impressed enough to invite an actor to audition for other projects. Attending a casting audition is a step up from the cattle call, especially for actors who do not have agents.

The difference between a cattle call and a casting audition is that a casting audition is not open to the public. Usually, actors get into casting auditions after their talent agents have made arrangements.[9] When an actor without an agent receives an audition invitation from a casting director, it should be taken seriously. Actors occasionally find out about casting auditions through word of mouth. When that happens, sending a resume and head shot to the casting director may also lead to an audition invitation. However the audition is arranged, it is very, very important that an actor show up on time.

An audition is basically a job interview, so being prepared and being professional are expected. Dress for the part when asked to before hand. Again: Be on time. Do not chew gum. Show confidence. Know the lines or be prepared to improvise. Actors who have learned the art of auditioning are most often the ones who get a callback.

Getting a callback means the casting director was impressed by the initial audition. For the actor, it means they did a good job and need to repeat that performance. During the callback—or second audition—top executives such as the producer, director, or writer may join the casting director.

As important as casting directors are for an actor's career, they usually do not have the final say on who gets cast. Their job is to recommend talented actors who they believe fit the role, but the top executives generally make the final decision.[10]

PRODUCERS AND DIRECTORS

Before giving their input on which actors to cast, a producer's first order of business is to find material to develop into a movie, made-for-television film, or production. This material, usually referred to as "property," can come from scripts, books, magazine

64

Audition Terms to Know

cold-reading: An unrehearsed reading of a scene.

mark: An area marked with tape, indicating where an actor performs.

sides: The portion of a script an actor is given to read dialogue from.

slate: A request for an actor to state their full name.

articles, and other sources. Locating a property is only the beginning for a producer. They hire the writers and the director, and they assemble the rest of the production staff. It is their job to oversee the entire movie-making process and supervise the crew. Producers also handle much of the day-to-day business aspects of filmmaking, which include securing financing and maintaining the production schedule.[11]

While the producer is involved with the business side of the film and television industry, the director's role focuses more on the creative process. Along with having their say at casting auditions, directors work closely with writers as scripts are developed. It is their job to transform the script and take their vision for the production to the screen. They do that by conducting rehearsals, working with the cast, advising set and costume designers, and making decisions about music, sounds, and special effects. Directors are the people who shout "Action" and

"Cut," but their duties go far beyond that. What appears on screen is a collaboration of many individuals but, ultimately, it is the director's vision.[12]

A number of very successful producers and directors in the industry have had experience doing both jobs. Several have become household names for the work they have done in the business. Some of the most recognizable producers and directors and a sample of their works include:

Steven Spielberg

Back to the Future, executive producer
E.T. the Extra-Terrestrial, producer and director
Jaws, director
Jurassic Park, director
Raiders of the Lost Ark, director
Schindler's List, producer and director
War of the Worlds, director

George Lucas

Indiana Jones and the Temple of Doom, executive producer
Raiders of the Lost Ark, executive producer
Star Wars, executive producer
Willow, executive producer

Ron Howard

A Beautiful Mind, producer and director
How the Grinch Stole Christmas, director
Splash, director

The Da Vinci Code, producer and director
Willow, director

WORKING WITH A TALENT AGENT

Because casting directors work closely with talent agents, actors increase their odds of finding work by signing on with a reputable agency. Actors with talent agents are able to get auditions that may not have been open to them otherwise. It is the talent agent's job to arrange meetings with casting directors and find auditions for their actors, but it is up to the actor to be on time and win the part. An assignment for the actor will result in the agent being paid a commission, or fee.

Once an actor is hired, the talent agent will negotiate a contract. Since agents work on commission—a percentage of their clients' earnings—it is in the agent's best interest to negotiate the very best contract on behalf of their clients. If an actor is not getting roles and not earning money, that means the agent is collecting zero commissions. Not too many business relationships can survive working without pay. The more money the actor makes, the greater the commission for the agent. The agent/client relationship is a business partnership and should be taken seriously.

Before sending out dozens of resume packages, do a little investigating and be sure that whoever is on the receiving end is legitimate. Ask for recommendations from other actors, teachers, or coaches. Be wary of con artists and scams that ask for money up front. Be suspicious of talent agents that advertise in newspapers or discover actors at the mall, beach, and other public venues.

The Screen Actors Guild (SAG) offers this advice on its Web site:

> We do not evaluate and/or recommend to members any service providers such as acting coaches, commercial workshops, modeling schools, photographers, or managers. There are so many people who want to be actors, that there are scam artists who will take your money and promise you acting jobs—but deliver nothing. Use the same common sense you would use in making other major purchases: i.e., network, check with the Better Business Bureau, don't pre-pay full amounts, compare prices.[13]

There are many laws that professional talent agents must abide by, and some states require them to be licensed. Before signing a contract with a talent agent, it is a good idea to know the laws in your area. Unions such as the SAG and the American Federation of Television and Radio Artists (AFTRA) have agreements with agents who are licensed to represent their union members. Talent agents who enter into these agreements are called franchised agents, and they are expected to follow union rules.

AFTRA's Web site states: "A 'franchised agent' is a person, firm or corporation that has entered into an agreement with AFTRA under which they agree to abide by certain rules and conditions when dealing with performers who work within AFTRA's jurisdiction. In most cities, AFTRA members are required to deal only with franchised agents for the purpose of securing and negotiating employment contracts."

Actors are not required to join a union unless they are hired to work on a union-regulated job. In general, union work offers better pay and working conditions than non-union work, so it can be advantageous for an actor to join. Franchised agents are able to refer actors to these higher-paying union jobs as well.

In 2002, SAG members rejected an agency franchise agreement with the Association of Talent Agents (ATA) and the National Association of Talent Representatives (NATR). Therefore, many talent agents lost their SAG-franchised status, and that had a direct impact on their clients. SAG recognized that those clients were caught in the middle, and a decision was made to suspend the SAG rule requiring members to deal only with franchised talent agents.

Even though talent agents who are affiliated with ATA and NATR are non-franchised, they are able to represent union members and find them work. SAG advises all actors "not to sign individual representation agreements if the terms provide less protection than Rule 16(g), the SAG Agency Franchise Agreement."[14] SAG offers listings of both franchised

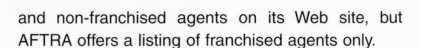

and non-franchised agents on its Web site, but AFTRA offers a listing of franchised agents only.

MAKING A LIVING

Having a successful career as an actor takes talent, determination, and a realization that every actor has to start somewhere. It is rare for a beginning actor to be cast after the first try. Typically, actors who are new to the business have to work their way up the ladder of success by taking on small roles. Every role, no matter how small, could potentially lead to larger roles.

As in every profession, there are different ranks and experience levels in acting. Beginning actors may have performed in plays or college films during their training or schooling, but they have not acquired an agent or union card. Actors with a few credits on their resume, union cards, and an agent have more credibility than a beginner, but are still lesser known than the actor who gets regular work. At these levels, and sometimes even higher, making a living can be a challenge.

The reality is that actors spend a lot of time—sometime years—taking on small parts before they are able to quit their day jobs. Knowing this up front is better than having it come as a surprise later. SAG offers this advice: "Despite the popular image that all actors are rich, most Screen Actors Guild members earn less than $7,500 per year from Screen Actors Guild jobs. It is almost certain that in your acting career there will be times when you will need to earn your living from work other than acting."[15]

WORKING YOUR WAY UP

While being an extra can be useful for earning credits and a SAG card, the pay is not enough to make a living. Beginning actors who work as extras—also referred to as background players—should consider the work to be a learning experience. Being a background player can offer insight into the business by seeing how actors, directors, producers, and crewmembers work together. Beginning actors need to soak up everything around them, learn how to network, and set goals.

Extras are used for movies, television series, soap operas, and commercials. The pay may vary depending upon the type of duty performed. Extra work is separated into three categories: Day extras are used to fill up the background and the work usually consists of standing in or walking around the scene. Special ability extras are cast to perform a skill such as swimming, bicycling, dancing, or any other special skill an actor has listed on a resume. Silent bit extras are the most sought-after extra positions. Actors who are assigned a silent bit role usually appear in scenes with the leading actors. Although they generally do not have lines, silent bit extras perform small on-screen parts such as waitresses, flight attendants, taxi drivers, or other minor characters who interact with the leading actors.[16]

Working as an extra may not be glamorous or high paying, but it can provide supplemental income. Considering the number of movies, TV series, and commercials made every year, actors who pursue being cast as an extra may find regular work.

Getting a part as day player or an under-five actor is a step above the standard extra role. A day player is an actor who is given a line. When an extra is needed to say a line, they are upgraded to day player status and receive a higher rate of pay. An under-five actor is someone who will have more screen time than the day player does. By speaking five lines or less, the under-five performer gains exposure, experience, better pay, and a nice credit for their resume.[17]

For any speaking role, an actor is bumped up the pay scale. According to contract terms covered by SAG and AFTRA, motion picture and television actors with speaking parts earned a minimum daily rate of $716 or $2,483 for a five-day week as of October 1, 2005. Even at those rates, most SAG actors earn less than $7,500 a year.[18]

Overall employment in the industry has grown at a steady pace, but the number of aspiring actors often exceeds the amount of available work. Even actors who are cast in speaking roles are subject to fluctuating employment. According to the 2006–2007 U.S. Department of Labor Occupational

Outlook Handbook: "Acting assignments typically are short term—ranging from one day to a few months—which means that actors frequently experience long periods of unemployment between jobs. The uncertain nature of the work results in unpredictable earnings and intense competition for even the lowest-paid jobs."[19]

CLIMBING THE LADDER OF SUCCESS

Some of the most successful actors are those who work regularly on films and television but who are not household names. Their faces are recognizable, and they play important roles. While they may not rank as high up as supporting or lead actors, working actors have established themselves in the business and make their living acting. They are true career actors. Casting directors call upon these working actors again and again to play specific characters.

Roles such as bad guy #1, crabby teacher, nurse, or other minor but important parts are usually cast with working actors. Lee Arenberg, who plays Pintel in the *Pirates of the Caribbean* movies, worked in the industry for years before landing that role. His long credit list includes playing characters named only Parking Attendant, Hold-up Man, and Demon. Viewers may recognize working actors but may not be able to put a name to their faces until they are cast in a larger role.

John C. Reilly, Leslie Bibb, and Will Ferrell in a scene from Talladega Nights: The Ballad of Ricky Bobby (2006).

Actors who are cast in supporting roles play their part next to the star of the film. Even though they do not have the leading role, they often share the spotlight with the star. John C. Reilly is the type of supporting actor who moviegoers probably recognize from other movies, but cannot put his name to his face. Reilly is one of Hollywood's busiest working character actors who is quickly becoming known for his comedy roles.

Fans of the 2006 movie *Talladega Nights: The Ballad of Ricky Bobby* saw Reilly play the part of Cal Naughton, Jr. Will Ferrell starred as Ricky Bobby but Reilly's role was important to the story and the overall comedic aspect of the movie.

Since 1989, Reilly has appeared in more than forty-five films and has also been seen on television. With his homegrown, rugged looks, Reilly has played a wide variety of characters. He is often at the top of casting agents' lists when they are looking to fill a supporting role. Janet Hirshenson, co-author of *A Star is Found*, states that Reilly is one of her favorite actors. When Hirshenson and Jenkins were casting the movie *The Perfect Storm*, Reilly immediately came to mind and was eventually cast as Dale Murphy.[20]

Like Dustin Hoffman, Reilly may not have the good looks of a leading man, but he can definitely hold his own when it comes down to acting ability. For his portrayal of Amos Hart in the movie musical *Chicago* (2002), both the Academy Awards and the Golden Globes nominated Reilly for Best Actor in a Supporting Role. Hirshenson summed up Reilly's career nicely when she wrote, "in the world of Names, John is one who teeters on the brink of being a star."[21]

At the top of the show biz ladder are the actors who are cast in supporting and leading movie roles. These actors are the A-List movie stars whose names are just as recognizable as their faces.

Movies that feature A-List actors usually end up being blockbusters that bring millions of dollars into the box office.

Only a select group of actors ever achieve this rank of stardom. Earning movie star status takes years of hard work and commitment. Actors may not necessarily aim for the A-List but find themselves at the top after their abilities and talents are recognized.

Playing the lead in a movie that brings in millions can almost guarantee an actor movie-star ranking. Actors whose films bring big bucks into the box office include Julia Roberts, Robert De Niro, Jim Carrey, Johnny Depp, and Reese Witherspoon.

Winning awards always catapults an actor into the spotlight. For big screen actors, winning an Oscar takes them to the very top level of fame. At the 2007 Academy Awards, actor Forrest Whitaker was awarded the top honor for his portrayal of Idi Amin in *The Last King of Scotland* (Fox Searchlight). He received an Oscar for best performance by an actor in a leading role. Whitaker was one of five actors nominated to win. The other 2007 nominees and their films were Leonardo DiCaprio in *Blood Diamond*, Ryan Gosling in *Half Nelson*, Peter O'Toole in *Venus*, and Will Smith in *The Pursuit of Happyness*.

Forrest Whitaker plays Idi Amin (center) in **The Last King of Scotland** *(2006).*

LEONARDO DICAPRIO: WORKING ACTOR TO A-LIST FAME

Leonardo DiCaprio's road to stardom began when he appeared on the children's television program *Romper Room*. As a youngster, DiCaprio also did commercials. In 1990, when he was sixteen years old, he got a part on the short-lived television series *Parenthood*. That same year, he made his daytime drama debut on the soap opera *Santa Barbara*. In 1992, the Young Artists Awards nominated him in

two categories: Best Young Actor Starring in a New Television Series for *Parenthood* and Best Young Actor in a Daytime Series for *Santa Barbara*.

DiCaprio's first big screen performance came in the 1992 movie *Critters 3: You Are What They Eat.* His fourth movie performance created quite a buzz in the industry. DiCaprio was cast with leading actor, Johnny Depp, in the 1993 film *What's Eating Gilbert Grape?* DiCaprio's portrayal of mentally challenged Arnie Grape was unforgettable. At age nineteen, he won the Best Supporting Actor award given by the

Leonardo Di Caprio (center, with Juliette Lewis and Johnny Depp) got his big dramatic break in What's Eating Gilbert Grape? *in 1993.*

National Board of Review. His performance in the supporting role also earned him nominations for both an Oscar and a Golden Globe.

DiCaprio earned a reputation for being low-key and avoiding the paparazzi. He had to get used to not being able to walk down the street unnoticed. "I really think I'm pretty well balanced for being in the position I'm in," he stated."[22]

By 1996, DiCaprio's hard work earned him the role as the leading man in the movie *Romeo and Juliet*, but it was the following year that Leonardo DiCaprio really became a household name. Playing Jack Dawson, the lead role in the 1997 mega-blockbuster *Titanic*, catapulted DiCaprio into celebrity status. Ten years later, Titanic held its spot as the highest-grossing film ever made, bringing in over $1.8 billion worldwide.

Between 1998 and 2006, DiCaprio starred in nine more movies, including *Gangs of New York* (2002), *Catch Me If You Can* (2002), *The Aviator* (2004), *Blood Diamond* (2006), and *The Departed* (2006). His lead performances in *The Aviator* and *Blood Diamond* brought Oscar nominations at the 2005 and 2007 Academy Awards. *The Departed*, in which DiCaprio played leading character Billy Costigan, won the Oscar for Best Motion Picture.

DiCaprio's determination and hard work proves that actors can work their way up the ladder of success and remain loyal to their roots. Recalling his background he said, "The last thing I want to turn

SELECTED MOVIE AWARDS

Academy Awards

Broadcast Film Critics Association Awards

Golden Globes

National Board of Review

People's Choice Awards

Screen Actors Guild Awards

into is a fat Hollywood jerk. I was brought up without much money and I was happy. I don't think that I will strive for money or success and end up greedy or big-headed. That only leads to unhappiness. I can still be down-to-earth and do this job as long as I enjoy it."[23]

His attitude is proof that enjoying the work is more important than any award. Even though awards recognize high achievement, thousands of talented, hard-working actors never receive them and still continue to act because the work itself is fulfilling and rewarding all on its own.

CAREER OPTIONS FOR THE WORKING ACTOR

Television offers a wide variety of opportunities for actors. The United States Department of Labor reports that the television industry is growing. According to the 2006–2007 Occupational Handbook, "Expanding cable and satellite television operations, increasing production and distribution of major studio and independent films, and continued growth and development of interactive media, such as direct-for-Web movies and videos, should increase demand for actors, producers, and directors."[1]

This should not imply that getting into television is easy. Actors who work on television learn their craft and receive their training the same way big screen actors do. And just like movie actors, television actors report to their sets to work with directors, producers, and other cast members. Even so, there are some differences between acting for television and acting in movies.

Recently, the popularity of reality shows on television networks and cable channels created a changed work environment for actors. With more and more reality shows taking up time slots, actors have fewer regular programs to audition for. While reality shows offer temporary acting jobs, the work has limited advancement potential.

PRIME TIME TELEVISION

In most time zones, prime-time programs air between 8:00 and 11:00 P.M. The majority of programs viewed during these hours are categorized in several genres such as action, adventure, animation, comedy, crime, drama, family, fantasy, mystery, reality, and more.

> GENRE—A type or category as in Western, Horror, Comedy.

An actor cast in a weekly television series is given the series guide—also known as a "bible" in the industry. The series guide outlines the show's premise and setting. It also gives background information about each character such as likes, dislikes, and quirks. Details on character relationships are provided as well.

> BIBLE—An industry term referring to the guide given to actors who work on series.

Unlike big screen movie actors who usually play a character as a one-time role, actors who work on series often find themselves portraying the same character for years until their show is canceled. For this reason, it is important for the TV actor to relate to the character on some level.

America Ferrera has this to say about playing Betty on the ABC series *Ugly Betty*: "I just fell in love with the character so much. I fell in love with who she is—the description of her personality and what she would go through and what she meant to the people around her."[2]

Speaking about the premise of the show and the character relationships, Ferrera added, "I find it particularly endearing. I think it's wonderful that the heroine of this show is the most unlikely and she's the one who doesn't have much to offer as far as appearance but she has so much more to offer on the inside. And then you have all of these people who are beautiful and polished and dressed to the nines and they're kind of ugly people on the inside."[3]

Like *Ugly Betty*, series plots generally center around one main character: the hero or heroine. The remaining cast of characters may include roles such as bad guy/villain, boss/co-worker, family members, friends, and various minor characters. Some series have an ensemble cast, meaning a group of actors share the main character slot.

REHEARSALS AND SCRIPTS

Programs that are taped before a live studio audience are particularly challenging. Actors on

America Ferrera in **Ugly Betty.**

these shows frequently improvise or ad-lib as they see fit or if they forget their lines. They must be prepared for anything to occur and be able to handle last-minute changes, even when they happen live. Actors who work in front of live audiences are trained to focus and try to stay in character. Every so often even the best-trained actors break character and show their real selves. Live audiences generally get a kick out of such character breaks.

Rehearsal schedules for television shows vary. Some shows that tape on the same studio set week after week have a more predictable schedule. Situation comedies typically rehearse for three or four days before filming. This allows sitcom actors to familiarize themselves with the script and memorize their lines. During final rehearsals, cast members may practice by doing a run-through, which allows them to perform the entire show without stopping.

> **RUN–THROUGH–**
> A rehearsal in which actors read their lines from beginning to end. Also known as a read-through.

Actors who work on action drama series need to know their scripted material before they are called to the set and filming begins. Because these shows shoot scenes on various locations, actors are called upon only when they are needed in a scene. Scenes for dramas are filmed out of sequence and the footage is edited later to create the final show.

THE SOAPS

Afternoon time slots are filled with soap operas that have stood the test of time. Soaps are extremely popular and have very loyal viewers. Many soaps have been on the air since the 1950s and have employed hundreds of actors each year, including extras and day players.

Soap opera actors have a reputation for being some of the hardest-working actors on television. Working on a soap is very fast-paced, but the demanding schedule is often rewarded with job security. Many veteran daytime actors, like Jacklyn Zeman, have built their careers by portraying a soap character. Viewers of *General Hospital* have been attached to Zeman's character, Bobbie Spencer, since 1977.

Because soap operas are daily programs, the actors have little preparation time with their scripts. Rehearsals generally take place in the morning, and the show is taped later in the afternoon.[4] With such a short amount of time to study a script, actors may forget one of their lines. To get around this and to help actors stay in character, soap operas use cue cards on their sets.

COMMERCIAL ACTING: PROS AND CONS

There are many opportunities for actors to find work on commercials. Advertising agencies hire casting directors to help search for just the right actors to promote their clients' products. Commercials are cast during open auditions as well as through agents who set up appointments for their qualified clients. Before auditions even begin, the agency and casting director may already have an idea of what type of actor would fit the role. A sixty-year-old actor with gray hair may be a perfect candidate for a commercial for health insurance but would not be a good spokesperson for the latest style of jeans.

Jackie Zeman (above) has played Bobbie Spencer on the daytime soap opera General Hospital *since 1977.*

Commercial roles are cast with a wide variety of actors. From the gorgeous actor promoting hair products to the guy-next-door actor promoting a fast-food chain, all ages, shapes, sizes, and ethnic groups are needed to sell products. Appearance and voice are key factors when casting directors decide who to call back and who to hire for the job.

Getting into commercials involves the same type of training as any other acting. There are additional courses and workshops that specialize in teaching skills that are unique to commercial actors. Some of the skills and techniques may include using cue cards, moving about while acting to the camera, and holding products without looking stiff. Students who take commercial classes may also practice another important aspect of auditioning—being natural. Natural body movements, gestures, voice, and inflection are skills that casting directors like to see.[5]

For the actor looking for steady employment, lucrative paychecks, and respectable work, commercial acting is an excellent career choice—especially for actors who make it their permanent employment goal. Many professional commercial actors have found success becoming the face behind a product.

Actors who aspire to move over to film or television should consider their long-term career goals before taking a lot commercial jobs. When actors become known because of the product they endorse, they risk being typecast or branded as "that fast-food girl" or "that cell phone guy." Because of this, industry executives caution commercial actors about starring in big advertising campaigns unless that is their top career goal. In that case, being typecast can be an advantage and lead to further commercial work.

The disadvantage of being branded is that once actors become known for their commercial work, it may be difficult for them to make the transition into film or television acting. Casting directors may not want to place an actor who has been seen over and over again on national commercials. The film and television audience may just recognize that actor and have difficulty accepting the person in a new role.[6] Actors should weigh their career goals carefully and consult with peers and professionals regarding the advantages and disadvantages of commercial work.

OPPORTUNITIES IN VOICE ACTING: THE VOICE-OVER ARTIST

Over the years, the need for voice-over artists has increased. Besides providing the voices behind animated characters in movies and television programs, voice artists also do TV and radio commercials. The expanding market of video and computer games has generated more jobs for voice-over artists, too. Some actors specialize in doing audio book narration—another growing opportunity for voice artists.

Income and pay scale vary depending upon what part of the country the commercial spot is broadcast and whether or not the performers are union members. AFTRA provides detailed wage information on its Web site and though member publications. For infomercials—advertising spots disguised as television programs—AFTRA wages which are valid through 2008 are:

On-Camera Performers or hosts
$1,134.20 for the first day of work and $567.10 for each additional day
Five Lines or Less (including models)
$534.65 per day
Off-Camera Announcers
$567.10 per four-hour session
Extras
$127.20 per day[7]

Because of the rising need for professional voice artists, competition in the field has grown. More and more celebrities are being hired for national radio commercial ads and to provide the voices of animated characters in movies such as *Shrek* and *Toy Story*.

Actors who aspire to become voice-over artists usually begin by working locally. Working with a voice coach and signing with a talent agency are helpful steps to take before going on auditions. Making a demo tape is a useful way for voice artists to hear themselves and hone their skills. It is also a necessary tool to have when looking for work. Instead of sending a head shot and resume, voice artists send their demo tapes to prospective employers and agents. The recordings on a demo tape should provide samples of an actor's ability to perform several voice styles.[8]

The most successful voice artists have a unique or special quality to their voice. Males with deep, authoritative voices and women with quirky or breathy voices seem to land the most work. Artists who have voices that are distinctive—not like any other—also do well.

ADDITIONAL JOB OPTIONS

The acting profession offers a wide variety of opportunities for actors, including working as stunt people, stand-ins, body doubles, music video performers, game show hosts, and models. Some actors perform on Broadway, in theater productions, or in theme parks. Employment is not limited to television, film, or radio, and actors who work hard can make it in show business.

6

ADVICE, EDUCATION, AND RESOURCES

Even though California and New York are considered the primary hubs of the film and television industry, work is available across the country. Many actors find jobs within their regions before making permanent moves to the East or West Coast. Relocating is not a must and it simply depends on an individual actor's goals. For actors who are willing to travel to auditions and find work, it is possible to live anywhere and still make a living.

Beyond the starring roles of television and film, actors have several employment options. Whether working as an extra, a day player, a soap opera cast member, or a commercial actor, actors with training, talent, and determination can find success.

Success has many levels and comes in many forms. It is important for aspiring actors to set realistic goals and understand that there is more to the acting profession than Hollywood, fame, and fortune. Getting into acting takes courage, confidence, and high self-esteem. Actors who prosper are the ones who feel driven to entertain. They take all the right steps and turn their dream of acting into a reality.

BE WISE, BEWARE: SCAMS AND CON GAMES

Aspiring actors are easy targets for unscrupulous crooks. The best way to be protected against falling victim to a scam or a con artist is by being informed

TEN STEPS TOWARD SUCCESS

Be on time.
Audition, audition, audition.
Have a really good headshot.
Keep a current resume.
Do not take rejection personally.
Make realistic goals.
Understand your strengths and weaknesses.
Learn from criticism.
Create a demo tape.
Continue taking courses and workshops.
Beware of scams and con games.

and educated. Be aware of how the industry works, and be wary of scammers who make offers that seem too good to be true. Be leery of anyone who promises overnight success.

Beware of phony agents. Legitimate agents will never ask for money up front.

Beware of fake casting directors. A real casting director will not charge a fee for an audition or screen test. Beware of "talent search" advertisements, especially if they are "one day only." These scammers bait wannabe actors, lure money out of their pockets, and are off to the next town before sunset.

Common sense and knowledge go a long way when weeding out suspicious characters from the real industry professionals. Online resources such as the Better Business Bureau and criminal court records are valuable tools for checking individual backgrounds and investigating whether or not a business is legitimate.

WORDS OF WISDOM
FROM WORKING ACTORS

Speaking about auditions, Robert De Niro (*Meet the Parents*, *Stardust*) advises: "As an actor who's starting out, you can't say, 'Hey, I'm too good for this.' You gotta do it, because people see you, your name gets around, and it has a cumulative effect. Auditions are like a gamble. Most likely you won't get the part, but if you don't go, you'll never know if you could've

A career in acting has many obstacles in it that must be overcome before success is achieved. Courage, confidence, and high self-esteem are needed for someone to take to the stage.

got it. I remember when I was in *Mean Streets*, I ran into Harvey Keitel in the Village—we were friends and he'd already been cast in the movie as Charlie. I had done a couple of leads in movies before so I said, 'Well, careerwise, I should be playing Charlie.' . . . I was saying it sincerely, but not in a way that was threatening to him. Then Harvey said, 'You know who you should play? Johnny Boy.' And that clicked.

Robert DeNiro and Harvey Keitel in Mean Streets *(1973).*

I played Johnny. Now I say to people, 'If you get a part, do it.' "[1]

In an interview with *Cinema Confidential*, actor Tom Hanks (*Big, Forrest Gump*) had this to say: "I think in the earlier days, acting is fun because the whole thing is like a big circus. Making movies is very glamorous; there's a lot of people around, there's a lot of attention, a lot of hoopla, you can go places that you've never been before. It's a blast [but] then you got to figure out that you're not here on vacation and that you actually have to do some work here at the same time. I have to say now, I think I'm in it for better reasons. I do the work that I think is absolutely fascinating. There's not nearly as much distraction for me now as there used to be."[2]

Speaking about dreams and reality, Raven-Symoné Pearman (*That's So Raven*) says: "If you put it out there in the atmosphere, it will come true, but you do have to work hard for it—you can't just sit on your behind and not do anything for it."[3]

Wesley Snipes (*Blade: Trinity*) offers this advise to aspiring actors: "They should be very versatile. Versatility is what's going to give them the longevity. The world is opening up and a lot more stories and a lot more interesting scenes to portray in film. Versatility will help them. They must be able to see the world, learn the world, and bring it to their craft."[4]

Josh Hutcherson, who stars in *Journey 3-D* (2008), *Firehouse Dog* (2007) and *Bridge to Terabithia* (2007), had this to say about handling

Wesley Snipes, N'Bushe Wright, and Stephen Dorff in a scene from Blade *(1998).*

peer pressure: "When I first started acting, I got a lot of crap from kids at school for it. They were being really mean. I didn't understand because I just loved doing it, and I didn't know what was wrong with it. It was hurtful to me, but I figured out after going through all of that, that you kind of have to let it go and just let them do that. Eventually, if you don't let it bother you, they'll stop because that's what they like. They like seeing you kind of getting all upset about it."[5]

EDUCATION AND TRAINING

The United States Department of Labor states:

> Formal dramatic training, either through an acting conservatory or a university program, generally is necessary, but some people successfully enter the field without it. Most people studying for a bachelor's degree take courses in radio and television broadcasting, communications, film, theater, drama, or dramatic literature.

AnnaSophia Robb and Josh Hutcherson in a key scene from Bridge to Terabithia *(2007).*

Actor Michael Morgan began his acting career as a child. As an adult, he has appeared on the television series *Law & Order: SVU* and has worked extensively onstage. His theater experience includes roles in *The Hobbit, Oklahoma!, Godspell, Macbeth*, and many more productions. In addition to performing in the Disney production of *Finding Nemo—The Musical*, Morgan has also played Zazu in the Broadway production of *The Lion King*. The following interview with Mr. Morgan was conducted via email by the author on March 5, 2007.

Q: What was your first audition experience? How did you prepare? What were you feeling?

A: I started performing in a community theater group when I was seven years old. Every kid got a part. So by the time I actually had to audition for a show, I already knew I could do it. I think this was a good way to start. My first real audition was for a musical in middle school. I remember being nervous; I still get nervous today. Nerves are good. They mean you care. I think I did very little to get ready. Sang a song and maybe read from the script.

Q: How have your auditioning experiences changed since then?

A: I still get nervous. Every time. I've done well over a hundred productions. Since then I learned I had to practice what I was going to do at the audition before I got there. Too often I would get in the audition room and fall apart with nerves. I also went to school and got a lot of onstage time. As a professional actor, my "job" is to audition, and the joy is getting the acting job. Now, when I audition, I will often go to five to six auditions a week (commercials, movies, Broadway musicals). In a year, I might book three or four jobs, and that is a good year (a theater job could last a year, and a commercial could be a few hours). In other words, you have to try and try again.

Q: How did you get your agent? Did you send a head shot/resume? Did they see you perform first?

A: At the end of my graduate acting school (I studied acting for three years after I finished college), the entire class of nine students presented a "showcase" in New York City and Los Angeles. We performed short scenes and sang a very small clip of a song. We invited casting directors and agents. At the end, the agents who were interested in us set up a meeting. Every major acting school does a showcase and agents tell me that this is the main way they get new talent. They get a flood of random mailings from actors but this way they can see what they will get before they commit. I met my agent though our showcase.

Q: What types of acting do you do (stage, screen, television, voice-over)?

A: I have done television, voice-over, theater and musical theater. Most of my work comes from the stage. But that is now. The jobs I get will change as I change. I feel that the older I get, the more TV I will do.

Q: What advice do you offer to actors who are looking to break into the business?

A: It is impossible to "break in" to acting. Most people who say they were "discovered" worked for years and years. The best way to start is to do anything you can get your hands on. Everything. School plays, community theater. One acting job leads to the next. The people you work for one place will lead you to more opportunities.

Q: Any additional comments you'd like to add?

A: There is a saying; "Only go into acting if you have no other choice." And it's true. It is miserable—the rejection and low pay. However, in my opinion, if you are meant to be an actor, absolutely nothing will stop you. And so many things, people, and institutions will try and keep you out. I remember when I started acting school I wanted the "secret handshake" that would open all the doors to the acting profession. And I found it. The "secret" is that there is no "handshake." No one really knows one way of doing any of it. And "it" is always changing.

Many [prospective actors] continue their academic training and receive a Master of Fine Arts (MFA) degree. Advanced curricula may include courses in stage speech and movement, directing, playwriting, and design, as well as intensive acting workshops. The National Association of Schools of Theatre accredits 135 programs in theater arts.

The National Association of Schools of Theatre (NAST) is an organization of schools, conservatories, colleges, and universities. NAST establishes national standards for undergraduate and graduate degrees and other credentials. As of 2007, more than 135 accredited educational institutions are NAST members.[6]

It is advisable to gather information when deciding upon obtaining further education. Visit campuses, read Web sites, write for brochures, talk to high school guidance counselors, and use government resources at state and local levels. The following is a partial list of colleges, universities, and institutes that offer courses and degrees in performing arts, drama, and acting.

Actors Studio (AS)
432 West 44th Street
New York, NY 10036

American Academy of Dramatic Arts (AADA)
Hollywood Campus
1336 North LaBrea Avenue
Los Angeles, CA 90028

New York Campus
120 Madison Avenue
New York, NY 10016
Web site: www.aada.org

American Musical and Dramatic Academy
(AMDA)
New York City Campus
2109 Broadway
New York, NY 10023

Los Angeles Campus
6305 Yucca Street
Los Angeles, CA 90028
Web site: http://www.amda.edu/

Boise State University
1910 University Drive
Boise, ID 83725-1565
Web site: www.boisestate.edu

Lee Strasberg Theatre and Film Institute
115 East 15th Street
Lee Strasberg Way
New York, NY 10003
Web site: www.newyork-strasberg.com

Northwestern University
1949 Campus Drive
Evanston, IL 60208
Web site: www.communication.northwestern.
edu/theatre

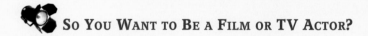

Stella Adler Studio of Acting
   31 West 27th Street, Third Floor
   New York, NY 10001
   Web site: www.stellaadler.com

University of Memphis
   Department of Theatre & Dance
   144 Theatre Communications Building
   Memphis, TN 38152-3150
   Web site: www.memphis.edu/theatre

University of Wisconsin—Whitewater
   800 West Main Street
   Whitewater, WI 53190-1790
   Web site: www.academics.www.edu/cac

Virginia Tech
   Department of Theatre Arts
   203 Performing Arts Building
   Blacksburg, VA 24061
   Web site: www.theatre.vt.edu

Selected Children's Theaters
There are hundreds of theaters around the United States that specialize in children's performances. A partial list is provided here and further information can be found through Internet searches and telephone directories.

Annenberg Center/Philadelphia
   International Theatre Festival for Children
   3680 Walnut Street
   Philadelphia, PA 19104

Web site: http://www.pennpresents.org/
events/childfest/

Children's Theatre Company
2400 Third Avenue South
Minneapolis, MN 55404
Web site: http://www.childrenstheatre.org/

First Stage Children's Theater
929 N. Water St.
Milwaukee, WI 53202
Web site: http://www.firststage.org/

Walden Family Playhouse
14500 West Colfax Avenue, Suite 600
Lakewood, CO 80401
Web site: http://www.waldenfamilyplayhouse.
com/aboutus/index.html

CHAPTER NOTES

CHAPTER 1. THE EVOLUTION OF ACTING

1. Justin Shenkarow, *Young Performers Page*, n.d., <http://www.sag.org/sagWebApp/application? origin=multipage_template.jsp&event=bea.portal. framework.internal.refresh&pageid=Hidden&cp=Agent Information&templateType=multipage&portletTitle= Young+Performers&contentType=Young+Performers& contentSubType=Links&contentUrl=/Content/Public/ youngperformers_welcome2.htm&idx=0> (August 20, 2006).

2. "Actors," *Encyclopedia of Careers and Vocational Guidance*, Thirteenth Edition, New York: Ferguson Publishing, Facts On File, Inc., *Career Guidance Center,* 2005, <www.fofweb.com> (August 31, 2007).

3. Ibid.

4. Joseph Ciolino, "Trivia for The Jazz Singer," *Internet Movie Database*, n.d., <http://www.imdb.com/ title/tt0018037/trivia> (August 20, 2006).

5. S. Mintz, "The Arrival of Sound," *Digital History*, 2003, <http://digitalhistory.uh.edu/historyonline/film_ chron.cfm> (September 7, 2007).

6. "The Talkies," *Time Magazine*, July 9, 1928, <http://www.time.com/time/magazine/article/ 0,9171,723496-2,00.html> (September 8, 2007).

7. "Silent Movies, Captions, and the Stars," *Let's Go to the Movies*, Museum of American Heritage, 2001, <http://www.moah.org/exhibits/archives/movies/ technology_development.html> (August 20, 2006).

8. Ibid.

9. Daniel Dopierala, "Harold Lloyd," *Internet Movie Database*, n.d., <http://pro.imdb.com/name/nm0516001/ bio> (August 20, 2006).

10. William Cahn, *The Laugh Makers: A Pictorial History of American Comedians* (New York: Bramhall House, 1957), Introduction.

11. George Stevens, Jr., *Conversations with the Great Moviemakers of Hollywood's Golden Age at the American Film Institute* (New York: Alfred A. Knopf, 2006), p. 12.

12. "Harold Lloyd," *Internet Movie Database*, n.d., <http://pro.imdb.com/name/nm0516001/personal> (August 20, 2006).

13. George Stevens, Jr., *Conversations with the Great Moviemakers of Hollywood's Golden Age at the American Film Institute*, Second Printing (New York: Alfred A. Knopf, 2006), p. 12.

14. Ibid., p. 12.

15. Charlie Chaplin, *My Autobiography Charles Chaplin* (New York: Simon and Schuster, 1964), p. 499.

16. Ibid., pp. 499–501.

17. "History of the Academy Awards," n.d., <http://www.oscars.org/aboutacademyawards/history01.html> (September 10, 2006).

18. Harry Gardiner, "Shirley Temple," *Cobblestone Magazine*, Vol. 28, Issue 1, January 2007, p. 47.

19. "Shirley Temple," *Internet Movie Database*, n.d., <http://pro.imdb.com/name/nm0000073/trivia> (September 10, 2006).

20. Ruth Stein, "Q & A With Shirley Temple," January 26, 2006, <http://www.shirleytemple.com/shirleyQNA.html> (September 10, 2006).

21. John Kenrick, "History of Musical Film 1927-1930: Part II," 2004, <http:www.musicals101.com/1927-30film2.htm> (September 10, 2006).

22. David Shipman, *Judy Garland: The Secret Life of an American Legend*, First Edition (New York: Hyperion, 1992), p. 29.

23. Noel Langley, Florence Ryerson and Edgar Allen Woolf, "The Wizard of Oz," *The Internet Movie Script Database*, n.d., <http://www.imsdb.com/scripts/Wizard-of-Oz,-The.html> (January 2, 2007).

24. Joe Morella and Edward Epstein, *Judy: The Films and Career of Judy Garland*, First Edition (New York: The Citadel Press, 1969), p. 162.

25. David Shipman, *Judy Garland: The Secret Life of an American Legend*, First Edition (New York: Hyperion, 1992), p. 116.

26. "American Comedy Awards, USA," *Internet Movie Database*, 1997, <http://pro.imdb.com/event/ev0000019/awards-1997> (October 12, 2006).

27. "A Brief history of the Oscar," n.d., <http://www.oscars.org/aboutacademyawards/awards/index.html> (October 12, 2006).

28. Hal Boedecker, "PBS, NBC profile trailblazing icons Sidney Poitier and Little Richard," *The Orlando Sentinel* (Fla.), January 11, 2000.

29. Steve Chagollan, "Lookback," *Daily Variety,* Volume 289, Issue 55/56, December, 15, 2005, p. 44.

30. Ibid.

Chapter 2. Pioneers of the Craft

1. David Sacks, "Theater in Ancient Greece," *Encyclopedia of the Ancient Greek World*, Revised Edition, Revised by Lisa R. Brody, New York: Facts On File, Inc., 2005, <www.fofweb.com> (November 7, 2007).

2. "Poetics, by Aristotle," n.d., <http://www.identitytheory.com/etexts/poetics.html> (November 19, 2006).

3. Lesley Adkins, Roy A. Adkins, "Thespis," *Handbook to Life in Ancient Greece*, Updated Edition, New York: Facts On File, Inc., 2005, <www.fofweb.com> (November 19, 2007).

4. "Constantin Stanislavky," *American Masters,* n.d., <http://pbs.org/wnet/americanmasters/database/stanislavsky_c.html> (November 7, 2006).

5. "Acting Quotes," n.d., <http://www.giga-usa.com/quotes/topics/acting_t004.htm> (November 9, 2006).

6. "History," n.d., <http://www.actors-studio.com/history/> (November 13, 2006).

7. Ibid.

8. "Actors Studio," *American Masters*, n.d., <http://pbs.org/wnet/americanmasters/database/actors_studio.html> (November 7, 2006).

9. "Strasberg," n.d., <http://actors-studio.com/strasberg/index3.html> (November 13, 2006).

10. Ibid.

11. "Method Acting," 2006, <http://www.jamactors.com/articles/method_acting.php> (November 13, 2006).

12. Denny Jackson, "Marilyn Monroe," *Internet Movie Database*, n.d., <http://pro.imdb.com/name/nm0000054/bio> (November 15, 2006).

13. Pete Martin, "Blonde, Incorporated," *Saturday Evening Post*, Volume 228, Issue 47, May 19, 1956, p. 177.

14. "Dustin Hoffman," n.d., <http://www.filmbug.com/db/1218> (November 20, 2006).

15. Janet Hirshenson and Jane Jenkins, *A Star is Found*, First Edition (Orlando: Harcourt, Inc., 2006), p. 131.

16. Ibid.

17. "Dustin Hoffman," *Internet Movie Database,* n.d., <http://pro.imdb.com/name/nm0000163/quotes> (November 20, 2006).

18. "Stella Adler," *American Masters*, n.d., <http://pbs.org/wnet/americanmasters/database/adler_s.html> (November 7, 2006).

Chapter 3. Modern Developments

1. "When Should I Join?" *Screen Actors Guild,* n.d., <http://www.sag.org/sagWebApp/application?origin=joinsag_template.jsp&event=bea.portal.framework.internal.refresh&pageid=JoinSAG&templateType=joinsag&portletTitle=null&contentType=null&contentSubType=When+Should+I+Join?&ln_idx=3> (November 11, 2006).

2. Rachel Green, "Dakota Fanning," *Internet Movie Database*, n.d., <http://pro.imdb.com/name/nm0266824/bio> (November 20, 2006).

3. Karen Valby, "The Most Powerful Actress in Hollywood is . . . Dakota Fanning," *Entertainment Weekly*, Issue 831, July 29, 2005, p. 10.

4. "Dakota Fanning," *Internet Movie Database*, n.d., <http://pro.imdb.com/name/nm0266824/quotes> (February 1, 2007).

5. Sid Smith, "Shucks, Tom Hanks Is Just a Likable Guy Who's Made a Splash in Movies," *Chicago Tribune*, July 27, 1986.

6. Todd McCarthy, "Auteur Opie," *Film Comment*, May-June 1984, p. 42.

7. "Big," *Internet Movie Database*, n.d., <http://pro.imdb.com/title/tt0094737/awards> (December 1, 2006).

8. Judy Fireman, ed., *TV Book: The Ultimate Television Book* (New York: Workman Publishing Company, Inc., 1977), p. 15.

9. Dick Moore, *Opportunities in Acting Careers* (Chicago: VGM Career Horizons, NTC/Contemporary Publishing Group, 1999), p. 89.

10. "AFTRA History," n.d., <http://www.aftra.com/aftra/whatis.htm> (December 5, 2006).

11. Judy Fireman, ed., *TV Book: The Ultimate Television Book* (New York: Workman Publishing Company, Inc., 1977), p. 81.

12. "Television and the Movie Industry," *Chronology of File History*, n.d., <http://www.digitalhistory.uh.edu/historyonline/film_chron.cfm#television> (December 10, 2006).

13. "History of Cable Television," n.d., <http://www.ncta.com/ContentView.aspx?contentId=2685> (December 10, 2006).

14. "2005 Annual Report and Member Resource Guide," 2005, <http://www.nab.org/Content/NavigationMenu/AboutNAB/2005AnnualReport.pdf> (December 10, 2006).

15. "Vanessa Anne Hudgens," *Internet Movie Database*, n.d., <http://pro.imdb.com/name/nm1227814/> (December 12, 2006).

16. Jessica Herndon, "Vanessa Hudgens Sounds Off," *People*, Volume 66 Issue 20, November 13, 2006, p. 49.

17. "Zac Efron," *Internet Movie Database*, n.d., <http://pro.imdb.com/name/nm1374980/> (December 12, 2006).

18. "About Equity," *Actors Equity Association*, 2006, <http://www.actorsequity.org/docs/about/aboutequity_booklet_06.pdf> (August 24, 2007).

19. Corbin Bleu, "Corbin Bleu," *Internet Movie Database*, n.d., <http://pro.imdb.com/name/nm0088298/bio> (December 12, 2006).

20. Edna Gunderson, "'High School,' the Musical," *USA Today*, February 27, 2006, <http://usatoday.com/life/movies/news/2006-02-27-high-school-musical_x.htm> (January 3, 2007).

Chapter 4. Show Business: What It Takes to Be a Working Actor

1. Joy Bennett Kinnon, "Raven Grows Up! From Cosby to the Big Screen to Disney," *Ebony,* May 2005, pp. 124–128.

2. Michael Saint Nicholas, *An Actor's Guide: Your First Year in Hollywood*, Revised Edition (New York: Allworth Press, 2000), p. 81.

3. Maurice Zolotow, "The Stars Rise Here," *Saturday Evening Post*, Volume 229, Issue 46, May 18, 1957, p. 83.

4. Ibid.

5. Larry Garrison and Wallace Wang, *Breaking Into Acting for Dummies* (New York: Wiley Publishing, Inc., 2002), p. 63.

6. Ibid., p. 67.

7. Mari Lyn Henry, Lynne Rogers, *How to be a Working Actor* (New York: Back Stage Books, 2000), p. 123.

8. Garrison and Wang, p. 120.

9. Ibid., p. 121.

10. Mari Lyn Henry, Lynne Rogers, *How to be a Working Actor* (New York: Back Stage Books, 2000), p. 98.

11. Fred Yager, Jan Yager, "Producer," *Career Opportunities in the Film Industry*, Facts on File, 2003, <www.fofweb.com> (January 5, 2007).

12. Fred Yager, Jan Yager, "Director," *Career Opportunities in the Film Industry,* Facts on File, 2003, <www.fofweb.com> (January 5, 2007).

13. "Getting Started as an Actor," n.d., <http://www.sag.org/sagWebApp/application?origin=faq_template.jsp&event=bea.portal.framework.internal.refresh&pageid=FAQs&templateType=faq&portletTitle=null&contentType=null&contentSubType=Getting+Started+as+an+Actor&ln_idx=5> (January 5, 2007).

14. "Agent Regulations," n.d., <http://www.sag.org/sagWebApp/application?origin=multipage_template.jsp&event=bea.portal.framework.internal.refresh&pageid=Hidden&cp=AgentInformation&templateType=multipage&portletTitle=Agent+Relations&contentType=Agent+Relations&contentSubType=Links&contentUrl=/Content/Public/AgentRelations_MemberAdvisory.htm&idx=2> (January 5, 2007).

15. "Getting Started as an Actor," *FAQ,* n.d., <http://www.sag.org/sagWebApp/application?origin=faq_template.jsp&event=bea.portal.framework.internal.refresh&pageid=FAQs&templateType=faq&portletTitle=null&contentType=null&contentSubType=Getting+Started+as+an+Actor&ln_idx=5> (February 20, 2007).

16. Garrison and Wang, pp. 206–207.

17. Michael Saint Nicholas, *An Actor's Guide: Your First Year in Hollywood*, Revised Edition (New York: Allworth Press, 2000), p. 39.

18. "Actors, Producers, and Directors," *Occupational Outlook Handbook*, 2006-07 Edition, Bureau of Labor Statistics, U.S. Department of Labor, <http://www.bls.gov/oco/ocos093.htm> (March 02, 2007).

19. Ibid.

20. Janet Hirshenson and Jane Jenkins, *A Star is Found,* First Edition (Orlando: Harcourt, Inc., 2006), p. 131.

21. Ibid., p. 124.

22. Angela Phinlay, "Leo," *Teen Tribute*, Volume 5, Issue 4, Winter 2002, p. 20.

23. "TW: Leonardo DiCaprio," *Rainbow Network*, December 26, 2004, <http://www.rainbownetwork. com/Fun/detail.asp?iData=22390&iCat=71&iChannel =20&nChannel=Fun> (July 24, 2007).

Chapter 5. Career Options for the Working Actor

1. "Actors, Producers and Directors," *Occupational Outlook Handbook*, 2006-07 Edition, Bureau of Labor Statistics, U.S. Department of Labor, <http://www.bls.gov/oco/ocos093.htm> (March 2, 2007).

2. "America Ferrera is Ugly Betty," *Entertainment Tonight Interview*, August 23, 2006, <http://www.

etonline.com/tv/fall2006/36827/index.html#> (February 20, 2007).

    3. Ibid.

    4. Michael Saint Nicholas, *An Actor's Guide: Your First Year in Hollywood*, Revised Edition (New York: Allworth Press, 2000), pp. 152–153.

    5. Larry Garrison and Wang, *Breaking Into Acting for Dummies* (New York: Wiley Publishing, Inc., 2002), p. 165.

    6. Ibid., p. 171.

    7. "AFTRA Informercial Agreement," October 30, 2006, <http://www.aftra.com/contract/infomercialrates.htm> (March 2, 2007).

    8. Garrison and Wang, p. 199.

CHAPTER 6. ADVICE, EDUCATION, AND RESOURCES

    1. Paul Mathur, "Robert De Niro to Paul Mathur in *Interview* November 1993," *Celebrity Profile: Robert Di Niro: EOnline,* n.d., <http://www.eonline.com/celebrities/profile/index.jsp?uuid=4553b5d0-43f9-4e59-a84f-0f4870d8b40a> (February 25, 2007).

    2. "Celebrity Profile: Tom Hanks," n.d., <http://www.eonline.com/celebrities/profile/index.jsp?uuid=4ddc31be-a18f-4c2e-b0bf-54a91910c86d> (February 25, 2007).

    3. Joy Bennett Kinnon, "Raven Grows Up! From Cosby to the Big Screen to Disney," *Ebony*, May 2005, pp. 124–128.

4. "Wesley Snipes," *Internet Movie Database*, n.d., <http://imdb.com/name/nm0000648/bio> (February 23, 2007).

5. Rebecca Murray, "Josh Hutcherson Lets His Imagination Go Wild in "Bridge to Terabithia," n.d., <http://movies.about.com/od/bridgetoterabithia/a/bridgejh021407.htm> (March 2, 2007)

6. "About NAST," n.d., <http://nast.arts-accredit.org/index.jsp?page=About+NAST> (March 4, 2007).

GLOSSARY

audition—An interview process in which an actor performs in front of casting personnel when trying out for a role.

bible—A guide given to actors who work on a series.

character—The role an actor takes on.

cue card—A board used off-camera to remind actors of their dialogue.

debut—An actor's first performance or the initial opening of a show.

demo tape—An audio or video recording used for promotion.

dialogue—Lines or spoken words in a script.

ensemble—A group of performers whose roles are equally important.

extra—A person used for non-principal roles; also known as background players.

genre—A type or category as in Western, Horror, Comedy.

improvisation—A performance without any preparation.

pantomime—To relay information or play a scene without using one's voice.

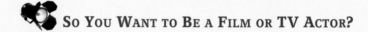

premiere—The first time a movie, film, or program is seen; the opening event.

principal—Any actor who has speaking lines.

rehearsal—A scheduled practice time used to read through scripts and act out scenes.

run-through—A rehearsal in which actors read their lines from beginning to end. Also known as a read-through.

script—The text of any performance which includes dialogue, action, and camera directions.

showcase—An organized event used to promote performers.

slapstick—A type of comedy that involves exaggerated movements and expressions.

stand-in—Actors who substitute for principal actors during off-camera shots.

stunt person—An actor who is specially trained to perform physically challenging or dangerous scenes.

troupe—A group of actors who travel together and perform as a company.

voice-over—Spoken dialogue performed by an actor who does not appear on-camera.

FURTHER READING

Adler, Stella. *The Art of Acting*. New York: Applause Books, 2000.

Gillespie, Bonnie. *Self-Management for Actors: Getting Down to (Show) Business*. Revised Edition. Hollywood, Calif.: Cricket Feet Publishing, 2006.

Hunt, Gordon. *How to Audition: For TV, Movies, Commercials, Plays, and Musicals*. New York: HarperCollins, 1995.

Jazwinski, Peter. *Act Now: A Step-By-Step Guide to Becoming a Working Actor*. New York: Three Rivers Press, 2003.

Rutter, Troy A. *Kids in the Biz: A Hollywood Handbook for Parents*. Portsmouth, N.H.: Heinemann, 2005.

INTERNET ADDRESSES

American Alliance for Theatre and Education (AATE)
http://www.aate.com/

Screen Actors Guild (SAG)
http://www.sag.com

Hollywood Creative Directory
http://hcdonline.com/

INDEX